Crossing the Plains

THEY STARTED FLIGHT

Crossing the Plains

A First Hand Narrative of the Early Pioneer Trail to California in 1857

William Audley Maxwell

LEONAUR

Crossing the Plains: a First Hand Narrative of the Early Pioneer Trail to California in 1857
by William Audley Maxwell

Leonaur is an imprint of Oakpast Ltd

Material original to this edition and
text presentation in this form
copyright © 2009 Oakpast Ltd

ISBN: 978-1-84677-654-0 (hardcover)
ISBN: 978-1-84677-653-3 (softcover)

http://www.leonaur.com

Publisher's Notes

Contents

Foreword

Diligent inquiry has failed to disclose the existence of an authentic and comprehensive narrative of a *pioneer* journey across the plains. With the exception of some improbable yarns and disconnected incidents relating to the earlier experiences, the subject has been treated mainly from the standpoint of people who travelled westward at a time when the real hardships and perils of the trip were much less than those encountered in the fifties.

A very large proportion of the people now residing in the Far West are descendants of emigrants who came by the precarious means afforded by ox-team conveyances. For some three-score years the younger generations have heard from the lips of their ancestors enough of that wonderful pilgrimage to create among them a widespread demand for a complete and typical narrative.

This story consists of facts, with the real names of the actors in the drama. The events, gay, grave and tragic, are according to indelible recollections of eye-witnesses, including those of the author.

W. A. M.
Ukiah, California
1915

CHAPTER 1

In Quest of the New

We left the west bank of the Missouri River on May 17, 1857. Our objective point was Sonoma County, California.

The company consisted of thirty-seven persons, including several families, and some others; the individuals ranging in years from middle age to babies: eleven men, ten women and sixteen minors; the eldest of the party forty-nine, the most youthful, a boy two months old the day we started. Most of these were persons who had resided for a time at least not far from the starting point, but not all were natives of that section, some having emigrated from Indiana, Kentucky, Tennessee and Virginia.

We were outfitted with eight wagons, about thirty yoke of oxen, fifty head of extra steers and cows, and ten or twelve saddle ponies and mules.

The vehicles were light, well-built farm wagons, arranged and fitted for economy of space and weight. Most of the wagons were without brakes, seats or springs. The axles were of wood, which, in case of their breaking, could be repaired *en route*. Chains were used for deadlocking the wheels while moving down steep places.

No lines or halters of any kind were used on the oxen for guiding them, these animals being managed entirely by use of the ox-whip and the "ox-word." The whip was a braided leathern lash, six to eight feet long, the most approved stock for which was a hickory sapling, as long as the lash, and on the extremity of the lash was a strip of buckskin, for a "cracker," which, when snapped by a practiced driver, produced a sound like the report of a pistol. The purpose of the whip was well understood by the trained oxen, and that implement enabled a skilful driver to regulate the course of a wagon almost as accurately as if the team were of horses, with the reins in the hands of an expert *jehu*.

An emigrant wagon such as described, provided with an oval top cover of white ducking, with "flaps" in front and a "puckering-string" at the rear, came to be known in those days as a "prairie schooner;" and a string of them, drawn out in single file in the daily travel, was a "train." Trains following one another along the same new pathway were sometimes strung out for hundreds of miles, with spaces of a few hundred yards to several miles between, and were many weeks passing a given point.

Our commissary wagon was supplied with flour, bacon, coffee, tea, sugar, rice, salt, and so forth; rations estimated to last for five or six months, if necessary; also medical supplies, and whatever else we could carry to meet the probable necessities and the possible casualties of the journey; with the view of travelling tediously but patiently over a country of roadless plains and mountains, crossing deserts and fording rivers; meanwhile cooking, eating and sleeping on the ground as we should find it from day to day.

The culinary implements occupied a compartment of their own in a wagon, consisting of such kettles, long-handled frying-pans and sheet-iron coffee pots as could be used on a camp-fire, with table articles almost all of tin. Those who attempted to carry the more friable articles, owing to the thumps and falls to which these were subjected, found themselves short in supply of utensils long before the journey ended. I have seen a man and wife drinking coffee from one small tin pan, their china and delftware having been left in fragments to decorate the desert wayside.

We had some tents, but they were little used, after we learned how to do without them, excepting in cases of inclement weather, of which there was very little, especially in the latter part of the trip.

During the great rush of immigration into California subsequent to 1849, from soon after the discovery of gold until this time, the usual date at which the annual emigrants started from the settlement borders along the Missouri River was April 15th to May 1st. The Spring of 1857 was late, and we did not pull out until May 17th, when the prairie grass was grown sufficiently to afford feed for the stock, and summer weather was assured.

At that time the boundary line between the "States" and the "Plains" was the Missouri River. We crossed that river at a point about half-way between St. Joseph and Council Bluffs, where the village of Brownville was the nucleus of a first settlement of white people on the Nebraska side. There the river was a half-mile wide. The crossing was effected by means of an old-fashioned ferryboat or scow, propelled by a small, stern-wheeled steamer. Two days were consumed in transporting our party and equipment across the stream; but one wagon and a few of the people and animals being taken at each trip of the ferryboat and steamer.

From the landing we passed up the west shore twenty miles, seeing occasionally a rude cabin or a foundation of logs, indicating the intention of pre-empters. This brought us to the town of Nebraska City, then a beginning of a dozen or twenty houses, on the west bank. Omaha was not yet on the map; although where that thriving city now stands there existed then a settlement of something over one hundred persons.

From Nebraska City we bore off north-westerly, sep-arating ourselves from civilization, and thereafter saw no more evidence of the white man's purpose to occupy the country over which we travelled.

There was before us the sky-bound stretch of undulat-ing prairie, spreading far and wide, like a vast field of young, growing grain, its monotony relieved only by occasional clumps of small trees, indicating the presence of springs or small water-courses.

Other companies or trains, from many parts of the coun-try, especially the Middle States, were crossing the Missouri at various points between St. Louis and Council Bluffs; most of them converging eventually into one general route, as they got out on the journey.

It is perhaps impossible to convey a clear understanding of the emotions experienced by one starting on such a trip; leaving friends and the familiar surroundings of what had been home, to face a siege of travel over thousands of miles of wilderness, so little known and fraught with so much of hardship and peril.

The earlier emigrants, gold-hunters, men only—men of such stuff as pioneers usually are made of—carried visions of picking up fortunes in the California gold mines and soon returning to their former haunts. But those who were going now felt that they were burning all bridges behind them; that all they had was with them, and they were going to stay.

Formerly we had heard that California was good only for its gold mines; that it was a country of rocks, crags and deserts; where it rained ceaselessly during half of the year and not at all in the other half.[1] But later we had been told that in the valleys there was land on which crops of wheat

1. As late as March, 1850, Daniel Webster said in the United States Senate: "Cali-fornia is Asiatic in formation and scenery; composed of vast mountains of enor-mous height, with broken ridges and deep valleys. The sides of these mountains are barren—entirely barren—their tops capped by perennial snow."

could be grown, and that cattle raising was good, on the broad acres of wild oats everywhere in the "cow counties." It was told us also that there were strips of redwood forest along the coast, and these trees, a hundred to several hundred feet in height, could be split into boards ten to twenty feet long, for building purposes; and that this material was to be had by anybody for the taking. Some said that the Spanish padres, at their missions in several localities near the Pacific shore, had planted small vineyards of what had come to be known as the "Mission" grape, which produced enormous crops. Another report told us that other fruits, including the orange and lemon varieties, so far as tried, gave promise of being valuable products of the valley and foothill soils. Such stories gave rise to a malady called "California fever." It was contagious, and carried off many people.

Our first camp was on the open prairie, where grass grew about four inches high, and a small spring furnished an ample supply of water. Firewood we had brought with us for that night. The weather was very fine, and all were joyous at the novelty of "camping out."

On or about the eighth day we came to the Platte River; broad, muddy stream, at some points a mile or more in width; shallow, but running rapidly, between low banks; its many small islands wholly covered by growths of cotton-wood trees and small willows. From these islands we obtained from time to time the fuel needed for the camp, as we took our course along the river's southerly shore; and occasionally added to the contents of the "grub" wagon by capturing an elk or deer that had sought covert in the cool shade of these island groves. Antelope also were there, but too wary for our huntsmen.

We forded the Platte at a point something like one hundred and fifty miles westward from its confluence with the Missouri. There was no road leading into the river, nor any

FORDING THE PLATTE CONSUMED ONE ENTIRE DAY

evidence of its having been crossed by any one, at that place. We were informed that the bottom was of quicksand, and fording, therefore, dangerous. We tested it, by riding horses across. Contrary to our expectations, the bottom was found to be a surface of smooth sand, packed hard enough to bear up the wagons, when the movement was quick and continuous. A cut was made in the bank, to form a runway for passage of the wagons to the water's edge; and the whole train crossed the stream safely, with no further mishap than the wetting of a driver and the dipping of a wagon into a place deep enough to let water into the box. Fording the Platte consumed one entire day. We camped that night on the north shore.

The train continued along the general course of the river about four hundred miles, as far as Fort Laramie, through open country, in which there was an abundance of feed for the animals, but where wood for fuel was scarce.

CHAPTER 2

A Solitary Emigrant

The Laramie and Sioux Indians were in those days the lords of that portion of the plains over which we travelled during the first several weeks.

They were fine specimens of physical manhood. Tall, erect, well proportioned, they carried themselves with a distinct air of personal importance and dignity. They had not taken to the white man's mode of dress. Each had, in addition to his buckskin breeches and moccasins, a five-point Mackinaw blanket, these comprising for him a complete suit. The blanket he used as an outer garment, when needed, and for his cover at night. Many of the more important "big injins" owned also a buffalo robe. This was the whole hide of the buffalo, with the hair on it, the inner side tanned to a soft, pliable leather, and the irregularities of its natural shape neatly cut away. It furnished the owner an excellent storm robe, sufficient protection, head to foot, in the severest weather.

The Indians of these tribes that we met were friendly, even to familiarity. One of them would approach an emigrant with a "glad-to-meet-you" air, extending a hand in what was intended to be "white-man" fashion. But "Mr. Lo" was a novice in the art of handshaking, and his awkwardness and mimicking attempts in the effort were as

WO–HAW–BUCK

amusing to us as satisfactory, apparently, to him. His vocal greeting, with slight variation from time to time, was in such words—with little regard for their meaning—as he had caught from the ox-driving dialect of the passing emigrants: "Wo-haw-buck," "Hello, John, got tobac?" If he added "Gimme biskit," and "Papoose heap sick," he had about reached the limit of his English vocabulary.

Large game was common along some parts of the way: buffalo, elk, antelope, deer, on the plains and hills; bear, mountain lions, wildcats and other species in the mountainous sections. They were shy and not easy to take, but we captured a few of some varieties. Some members of the party demonstrated that fishing was good in the Rocky Mountain streams. Naturally the men were hopeful of securing specimens of the larger game, but our lack of experience and scarcity of proper equipment for the purpose were against the chance, though not to the extent of our entire disappointment.

Only persons of much experience on the plains could form even an approximate estimate of the great number of buffaloes sometimes seen together. It has been stated that there were herds numbering more than fifty thousand. Such an aggregation would consume days in passing a given point, and in case of a stampede, all other animals in its path were doomed to destruction. A herd of buffaloes quietly grazing was sometimes difficult to distinguish, when viewed from a considerable distance, from a low forest; their rounded bodies and the neutral tint of their shaggy coats giving them the appearance of bushes.

When the train was nearing the fork of the Platte River a herd of buffaloes was seen, quietly grazing on the plain, a mile or more to the right, beyond a small water-course.

Deciding we would try our prowess, Captain Maxwell and this narrator rode to the creek, at a point some distance below the position of the herd, where we tied our horses, then crept along, under cover of the creek bank, till we had gone as near as possible, without being seen by the herd, distant from us not much more than a hundred yards.

Cautiously peering above the edge of the bank, we selected a choice buffalo among those nearest us, and both fired. The entire herd galloped wildly away, continuing till all passed from view over a hill some miles northward. Not one showed sign of having been hit.

As we were about to leave the place, what should we see but a lonely buffalo, coming down the slope toward where we were, moving with leisurely tread and manner perfectly unconcerned. Notwithstanding our recent firing, this animal evidently had no suspicion of our presence. We remained and awaited his coming.

He walked a few steps, then browsed a little, as if in no hurry about anything. Captain John and I felt our hope rise; we laid our plans and waited patiently.

Just where the buffalo trail led down the bank of the creek, there were, as in many places near the stream, some scattered cottonwood and other trees. One of these that once stood on the brink had fallen till its top caught in the fork of another tree, and rested at a gentle incline upward from where it had grown. At the roots of this fallen tree we concealed ourselves, to wait, hoping that the big animal would come down to the water, but a few yards from us; for we guessed that he was one that had not yet had his drink from the brook that day, and was determined not to leave until he slaked his thirst.

It was an anxious while of waiting, but not long. I was fearful that my hard-thumping heart-beats would be audible and frighten him away. Could it be true that I had an attack of "buck-ague"? Perish the thought.

Finally his bovine majesty came lazily over the top of the

FROM OUR COIGN OF VANTAGE WE CONTINUED TO SHOOT

bank, with a heavy, slow motion; grunting and puffing, as if he were almost too heavy for his legs. When he got to the bottom of the bank and was about to drink, Captain John whispered our agreed signal: "One, two, three;" we fired, simultaneously, and repeated. The big fellow stood still for a moment after the shots and looked about, with a slow movement and stolid gaze, turning his head questioningly from side to side, as if he would say, "I thought I heard something pop."

Somehow we knew we had hit him, and we wondered why he did not fall. His little, black eyes rolled and glinted under his shaggy foretop. Then he seemed to swell; crouching slightly, as does a beast of prey when about to spring; lowered his head, pawed the earth and shook his mane. His whole body became vibrant with the obvious desire to fight,— and no antagonist in sight. Uttering a tremendous grunt, he arched his back again, stamping with all four feet, somewhat like the capers of a Mexican bronco when preparing to buck"; then he snorted once more, with such explosive force as seemed to shake the tree beside which we were hidden, as he looked about for something to pitch into.

By this time we thought we understood why a kind Providence had caused that cottonwood tree to lodge at such an angle that a buffalo could not climb it, but we could—and we did. Getting ourselves safely into the fork of the tree, we continued to shoot from our coign of vantage till the big fellow dropped. When he ceased to kick or give any sign of belligerency, we came down and approached him, carefully. Then we dressed him, or as much of him as we could carry in two bags that we had strapped behind our saddles, and rejoined the train after our people had gone into camp for the night.

We had our first buffalo steak for supper that night. We also had the satisfaction of observing signs of jealousy on the part of the other men who had never killed a buffalo.

CHIMNEY ROCK

One of the first natural curiosities we saw was Chimney Rock; a vertical column of sandstone something like forty feet high, with a rugged stone bluff rising abruptly near it. Its appearance, from our distant view, resembled a stone chimney from which the building had been burned away, as it stood, solitary on the flat earth at the south side of the Platte River, we travelling up the north shore. Such a time-chiselled monument was a novelty to us then. To the early emigrants it was the first notable landmark.

While some distance farther west, as we scaled the higher slopes, we could see to the southward the snow-capped peaks of that region which long afterward was taken from western Nebraska to become the Territory of Colorado, and later still, the State of that name. Looking over and past the locality where, more than a year thereafter, the town of Denver was laid out, we saw, during several weeks, the summit of Pike's Peak, hundreds of miles away.

One evening when we were going into camp we were overtaken by a man trundling a push-cart. This vehicle had between its wheels a box containing the man's supplies of food and camp articles, with the blankets, which were in a roll, placed on top; all strapped down under an oilcloth cover.

With this simple outfit, pushed in front of him, this man was making his way from one of the Eastern States to California, a distance of more than three thousand miles. He was of medium size, athletic appearance, with a cheerful face. He visited us overnight. The next morning he was invited to tie his cart behind one of our wagons and ride with us. He replied that he would be pleased to do so, but was anxious to make all possible speed, and felt that he could not wait on the progress of our train, which was somewhat slower than the pace he maintained. It was said that he was the first man who made the entire trip on foot and alone, from coast to coast, as we were afterwards informed he succeeded in doing.

From time to time the tedium was dispelled by varied incidents; many that were entertaining and instructive, some ludicrous, some pathetic, and others profoundly tragic. Agreeable happenings predominated largely during the early stages, and those involving difficulties and of grave import were mainly a part of our experiences toward the close of the long pilgrimage. Such an order of events might be presumed as a natural sequence, as the route led first over a territory not generally difficult to travel, but farther and farther from established civilization, into rougher lands, and toward those regions where outlawry, common to all pioneer conditions, was prevalent.

With our company were four or five boys and young men, eighteen to twenty-one years of age, also a kindly and unpretentious but droll young fellow, named John C. Aston, whose age was about twenty-five. This younger element was responsible for most of the occurrences of lighter vein, which became a feature of our daily progress.

Aston's intimate friends called him "Jack," and some of the more facetious ones shortened the cognomen "Jack Aston" by dropping the "ton," inconsiderately declaring that the briefer appellation fitted the man, even better than did his coat, which always was loose about the shoulders and too long in the sleeves. But all knew "Jack" to be an excellent fellow. His principal fault, if it could be so termed, was a superabundance of good-nature, a willingness at all times to joke and be joked. He had a fund of stories—in some of which he pictured himself the hero—with which he was wont to relieve the tedium of the evening hours. A violin was among his effects, which he played to accompany his singing of entertaining countryside songs. Most of these were melodious, and highly descriptive. "Jack" had much music in his soul, and sang with good effect.

There was one melody that he sang oftenest, and sang

from the heart—one that was rendered nightly, regardless of any variation in the program; a composition that embraced seventeen verses, each followed by a soothing lullaby refrain; a song which, every time he sang it, carried "Jack" again to his old home in the Sunny South, and seemed to give him surcease from all the ills of life. Of that song a single verse is here reproduced, with deep regret that the other sixteen are lost, with all except a small fraction of the tune. Yet, cold, inanimate music notes on the paper would convey, to one who never heard him sing them, only the skeleton; the life, sympathy and soul of the song would be lacking. We needed no other soporific. Here it is:

> *Oh, the days of bygone joys,*
> *They never will come back to me;*
> *When I was with the girls and boys,*
> *A-courting, down in Tennessee.*
> *Ulee, ilee, aloo, ee—*
> *Courting, down in Tennessee.*

It was "Jack's" habit to allow his head to hang to the

left, due, presumably, to much practice in holding down the large end of his violin with his chin. He was prone to sleep a great deal, and even as he sat in the driver's seat of a "prairie-schooner," or astride a mule, the attitude described often resulted in his being accused of napping while on duty. The climatic conditions peculiar to the plains, and the slow, steady movement of the conveyances, were conducive to drowsiness, in consequence of which everybody was all the time sleepy. But "Jack" was born that way, and the very frequent evidences of it in his case led to a general understanding that, whenever he was not in sight, he was hidden away somewhere asleep.

"Jack's" amiability, too, was a permanent condition. Apparently no one could make him angry or resentful. For this reason, he was the target for many pranks perpetrated by the boys. Like this:

One evening "Jack" took his blanket and located for the night at a spot apart from the others of the company, under a convenient sage bush. The next morning he was overlooked until after breakfast. When the time came for

HAULED THE DELINQUENT OUT

24

hitching the teams, he was not at his post. A search finally revealed him, still rolled in his bedding, fast asleep. When several calls failed to arouse him, one of the boys tied an end of a rope around "Jack's" feet, hitched a pair of oxen to the other end, and hauled the delinquent out some distance on the sand. "Jack" sat up, unconcernedly rubbed his eyes, then began untying the rope that bound his feet, his only comment being—

"Ulee, ilee, aloo, ee;

"Courting, down in Tennessee."

CHAPTER 3

Devil's Gate

At Fort Laramie we left the Platte River, and, bearing north-westerly, entered the Black Hills, a region of low, rolling uplands, sparsely grown with scrubby pine trees; the soil black, very dry; where little animal life was visible, excepting prairie dogs.

There may be readers who, at the mention of prairie dogs, see mentally a wolf or other specimen of the *genus canis*, of ordinary kind and size. The prairie dog, however, is not of the dog species. It bears some resemblance to a squirrel and a rat, but is larger than either. It may be likened to the canine only in that it barks, somewhat as do small dogs. Prairie dogs live in holes, dug by themselves. Twenty to fifty of these holes may be seen within a radius of a few yards, and such communities are known to plains people as "towns." On the approach of anything they fear the little fellows sit erect, look defiant and chatter saucily. If the intruder comes too near, the commanding individual of the group, the mayor of the town, so to speak, gives an alarm, plainly interpreted as, "Beware; make safe; each man for himself," and instantly each one turns an exquisite somersault and disappears, as he drops, head downward, into the hole beside him.

John L. Maxwell had made the trip over the plains from

the Missouri River to California in 1854, returning, via Panama, in 1856, to take his family to the West, accompanying the train of his elder brother, Dr. Kennedy Maxwell. He was of great service to us now, by reason of his experience and consequent knowledge of the country traversed. He was therefore elected to act as pilot of the company, with the title "Captain John," which clung to him for many years.

The emigrant trail in some parts of the way was well marked. In other places there was none, and we had to find our way as best we could, not always without difficulty. Often Captain John and others would ride ahead of the train a considerable distance, select routes for passage through places where travel was hard or risky, choose camp-sites, and, returning, pilot the train accordingly.

At various times, despite every care in selecting the route, the train went on a wrong course, and at least once was completely astray. This was one morning as the company was passing out of the Black Hills country. Information had been received that at this place a short-cut could be made which would save fifteen or twenty miles. There were no marks on the ground indicating that any train ahead had gone that way, but the leaders decided to try it. This venture led the company into a situation not unlike the proverbial "jumping-off place."

Directly in our course was a declivity which dropped an estimated depth of sixty to one hundred feet below the narrow, stony flat on which we stood, down into a depressed valley. Abrupt ridges of broken stone formation were on our right and left, inclosing us in a small space of barren, waste earth. The elements had crumbled the rocks down for ages, until what perhaps had been once a deep canyon was now a narrow flat, a mass of debris, terminating at the top of the steep, ragged cliff that pitched downward before us. The high, rocky ridges on both sides were wholly impassable, at least for the teams. A search finally disclosed, at the base of the ridge on our right, a single possible passage. It was narrow, slightly wider than a wagon, and led downward at a steep incline, into the valley below, with rocks protruding from both its side walls, its bottom strewn with stones such as our vehicles could not pass over in an ordinary way.

We were confronted with the problem how to get the wagons down that yawning fissure; the alternative being to retrace our steps many miles.

At the bottom of this cliff or wall that barred our way could be seen a beautiful valley, stretching far and wide away to the northwest; a scene of enchanting loveliness, a refreshing contrast to the dry and nearly barren hills over which we had travelled during the many days last past. A short distance from the foot of the wall was a small stream of clear water, running over the meadow-flat. Rich pasture extended along the line of trees that marked the serpentine course of the brook which zigzagged its way toward the southwest. Every man, woman and child of our company expressed in some way the declaration, "We *must* get into that beautiful oasis." It looked like field, park and orchard, in one landscape; all fenced off from the desolate surroundings by this wall of stone. Like Moses viewing Canaan from Nebo's top, we looked down and yearned to be amidst its freshness.

It was not decreed that we should not enter in. A little distance to the south, near the other ridge, we discovered another opening, through which the animals could be driven down, but through which the wagons could not pass. This was a narrow, crooked ravine, and very steep; running diagonally down through the cliff; a sort of dry water-way, entirely bridged over in one part by an arch of stone, making it there a natural tunnel or open-ended cave; terminating at the base of the cliff in an immense doorway, opening into the valley.

The teams were unhitched from the wagons, the yokes taken off the oxen, and all the cattle, horses and mules were driven through the inclined tunnel into the coveted valley. The women and children clambered down, taking with them what they could of the camp things, for immediate use, and soon were quite "at home" in the valley, making free use of the little creek, for whatever purposes a little creek of pure, cold, fresh water is good, for a lot of thirsty, dust-covered wayfarers.

The puzzle of getting the wagons down next engrossed the attention of our best engineers. The proposition to unpack the lading, take the wagons apart, and carry all down by hand, appeared for a time to be the only feasible plan. Captain John, however, suggested procuring rope or chain about one hundred feet in length, for use in lowering the wagons, one at a time, through the first-mentioned passage. Sufficient

THE WAGONS WERE LOWERED THROUGH THE CREVICE

rope was brought, one end fastened to the rear axle of a wagon, the other end turned around a dwarf pine tree at the top of the bluff; two men managed the rope, preventing too rapid descent at the steeper places, while others guided the wheels over the stones, and the wagon was lowered through the crevice, with little damage. Thus, one by one, all the wagons were taken into the valley before the sun set.

It was a happy camp we had that night; though every man was tired. There was wood for fire, and a supply of good water and pasture sufficient for dozens of camps. Some one ventured the opinion that the Mormon pioneers had over-looked that spot when seeking a new location for Zion.

Except that it was very pleasant to inhabit, we knew little of the place we had ventured into, or its location. How we were to get out did not appear, nor for the time being did this greatly concern us; and soon after supper the camp was wrapped in slumber, undisturbed by any coyote duet, or, on this occasion, even the twitter of a night bird.

We did not hurry the next morning, the inclination being to linger awhile in the shady grove by the brook side. With a late start, the day's travel took us some twelve miles, through and out of the valley, to a point where we made the best of a poor camping place, on a rough, rocky hillside. The following day there was no road to follow, nor even a buffalo trail or bear path; but by evening we somehow found our way back into the course usually followed by emigrants, not knowing whether the recent detour had lessened or increased the miles of travel, but delighted with the comfort and diversion afforded by the side-ride. Thinking that others, seeing our tracks, might be led into similar difficulties, and be less fortunate perhaps in overcoming them, two of our young men rode back to the place of divergence, and erected a notice to all comers, advising them to "Keep to the right."

Another freak of Nature in which we were much interested was the "Devil's Gate," or "Independence Rock," where we first came to the Sweetwater River, in Wyoming. This is a granite ridge, some two hundred feet in length, irregular in formation and height, resembling a huge molehill, extending down from the Rocky Mountain heights and being across the river's course; the "Gate" being a vertical section, the width of the stream, cut out of a spur of Rattlesnake Mountain. If his Satanic majesty, whose name it bears, had charge of the construction, apparently he intended it only as a passage-way for the river, the cut being the exact width of the river as it flows through. The greater part of the two walls stand two hundred and fifty feet high, above the river level, perpendicular to the earth's plane, facing each other, the river between them at the base. Many names had been cut in the surface of the rock, by passing emigrants.

We stopped for half a day to view this extraordinary scene. Some of the boys went to the apex, to see if the downward view made the rock walls appear as high as did the upward view: and naturally they found the distance viewed downward seemed much greater. Our intention was to stand on the brink and experience the sensation of looking down from that great height at the river. The face of the wall where it terminates at the top forms an almost square corner, as if hewn stone. A few bushes grew a short distance from the edge, and as we approached the brink there was a sense of greater safety in holding onto these bushes. But while holding on we could not see quite over to the water below. We formed a chain of three persons, by joining hands, one grasping a large bush, that the outer man might look over the edge—if he would. But he felt shaky. He was not quite sure that the bush would not pull up by the roots, or one of the other fellows let go. For sometime no one was willing to make a real effort to look over the

edge, but finally "Jack" said he would save the party's repu-
tation for bravery, by assuming the role of end-man. He
made several bold approaches toward the edge, but each
time recoiled, and soon admitted defeat. "Boys," said he,
"I'm dizzy. I know that 'distance lends enchantment'; I'll
get back farther, take the best view I can get, and preserve
the enchantment." To cover his discomfiture, he started for
camp, whistling: "Ulee, ilee, aloo, ee."

The next excursion off the route in search of novelty was on a clear afternoon a few days after passing the
"Devil's Gate," when three young fellows decided to take
a tramp to the rock ridge lying to our right. We hoped to
find some mountain sheep. From the Sweetwater River to
the ridge was apparently half a mile, across a grassy flat. We
knew that the rare atmosphere of that high altitude often
made distances deceiving, and determined to make due al-
lowances. Having crossed the river and being ready for a
sprint, each made a guess of the distance to the foot of the
rock ridge. The estimates varied from two hundred yards to
three hundred. Off we went, counting paces. At the end of
three hundred we appeared to be no nearer the goal than
when we started. The guesses were repeated, and when we
were about completing the second course of stepping, making nearly six hundred yards in all, one of the boys espied a
mountain sheep on the top of the ridge, keeping lookout,
probably, for the benefit of his fellows, feeding on the other
side, as is the habit of these wary creatures.

With head and great horns clearly outlined on the back-
ground of blue sky, he was a tempting target. Without a
word, the three of us levelled guns and fired. Mr. Mountain
Sheep stood perfectly still, looking down at us. We could
not see so much as the winking of an eye. Making ready
for another volley, we thought best to get nearer; but as we
started the head and horns and sheep disappeared behind

the top of the ridge. Further stepping proved that we had shot at the animal from a distance of at least half a mile. Our guns were good for a range of two hundred yards, at most.

Much of the time, especially while in the higher mountains, we were in possession of little knowledge of our position. There were no marks that we observed to indicate geographical divisions, and we had no means for determining many exact locations, though some important rivers and prominent mountain peaks and ridges were identified. We knew little, if anything, then of territorial boundaries, and thought of the country traversed as being so remote from centres of civilization—at that time but little explored, even—that we could not conceive any object in attempting to determine our location with reference to geographical lines; nor could we have done so except on rare occasions. Our chief concern was to know that we were on the best route to California.

We crossed the summit of the Rocky Mountains by the South Pass. Though it was July, the jagged peaks of the Wind River Mountains bore a thick blanket of snow. Sometime after leaving the "Devil's Gate" we passed Pacific Springs. There we gained first knowledge that we had passed the summit, on observing that the streams flowed westerly. Patient plodding had now taken us a distance of actual travel amounting to much more than one thousand miles and, from time to time, into very high altitudes. About four miles west of Pacific Springs we passed the junction of the California and Oregon trails, at the Big Bend of the Bear River.

Green River, where we first came to it, was in a level bit of country. There this stream was about sixty yards wide; the water clear and deep, flowing in a gentle current. For the accommodation of emigrants, three men were there, operating a ferry. Whence they came I do not remember, if they told us. We saw no signs of a habitation in which they might have lived. The ferrying was done with what was really a raft of logs, rather than a boat. It was sustained against the current by means of a tackle attached to a block, rove on a large rope that was drawn taut, from bank to bank, and was propelled by a windlass on each bank. When a wagon had been taken aboard this cable ferry, the windlass on the farther side was turned by one of the men, drawing the raft across. After unloading, the raft was drawn back, by operation of the windlass on the opposite shore, where it took on another load. The third man acted as conductor, collecting a toll of three dollars per wagon. All the horses, mules and cattle were driven into the river, and swam across.

The company passed along the shore of the Green River, down the Big Sandy River and Slate Creek, over Bear River Divide, then south-westward into Utah Territory.

CHAPTER 4

Rumours of Redmen

Soon after passing the summit of the Rocky Mountains there were rumours of a hostile attitude toward emigrants on the part of certain Indian tribes farther west. For a time such information seemed vague as to origin and reliability, but in time the rumours became persistent, and there developed a feeling of much concern, first for the safety of our stock, later for our own protection.

Measures of precaution were discussed. Men of our train visited those of others, ahead and behind us, and exchanged views regarding the probability of danger and the best means for protection and defence. We were forced to the conclusion that the situation was grave; and the interests of the several trains were mutual. As the members of the different parties, most of whom previously had been strangers to one another, met and talked of the peril which all believed to be imminent, they became as brothers; and mutual protection was the theme that came up oftenest and was listened to with the most absorbing interest.

By the time we had crossed the Green River these consultations had matured into a plan for consolidation of trains, for greater concentration of strength. A. J. Drennan's company of four or five wagons, immediately ahead of us, and the Dr. Kidd train, of three wagons, next behind us, closed up the space between, and all three travelled as one train. Thus combined, a considerable number of able-bodied men were brought together, making a rather formidable array for an ordinary band of Indians to attack. Every man primed his gun and thenceforth took care to see that his powder was dry.

Still the youthful element occasionally managed to extract some humour out of the very circumstances which the older and more serious members held to be grounds for forebodings of evil. One morning after we had left camp, a favourite cow was missing from the drove. "Jack" Aston and Major Crewdson, both young fellows, rode back in search of the stray. From a little hill-top they saw, in a ravine below, some half dozen Indians busily engaged in skinning the cow. "Jack" and the Major returned and merely reported what they had seen. They were asked why they had not demanded of those "rascally" Indians that they explain why they were skinning a cow that did not belong to them. "Jack" promptly answered that, as for himself, he had never been introduced to this particular party of Indians, and was not on speaking terms with them; furthermore, neither he nor the Major had sufficient knowledge of the Indian language properly to discuss the matter with them.

The route pursued led to the north of Great Salt Lake, thence north-westerly. Our line of travel did not therefore bring us within view of the Mormon settlements which had already been established at the southerly end of the great inland sea.

We camped one night approximately where the city of Ogden now stands, then a desolate expanse of sand-dunes. A group of our men sat around the camp-fire that evening, discussing the probability of a railroad ever being constructed over the route we were travelling. All of them were natives or recent residents of the Middle West, and it is probable that not one had ever seen a railroad. The unanimous opinion was that such a project as the building of a railroad through territory like that over which we had thus far travelled would be a task so stupendous as to baffle all human ingenuity and skill. Yet, some twelve years later, the ceremony of driving the famous "last spike," completing the railroad connection between the Atlantic and Pacific, was performed on a sand flat very near the spot where we camped that night. The intervening period saw the establishment of the "pony express," which greatly facilitated the mail service (incidentally reducing letter postage to Pacific Coast points from twenty-five to ten cents). That service continued from the early sixties until through railroad connection was made.

After the consolidation of trains as described, our next neighbour to the rear was Smith Holloway, whose "outfit" consisted of three wagons, with a complement of yoke-wise oxen and some horses and mules; also a large drove of stock cattle, intended for the market in California, where it was known they would be saleable at high prices. He had with him his wife, a little daughter, and Jerry Bush, Mrs. Holloway's brother, a young man of twenty-one years; also two hired men, Joe Blevens and Bird Lawles. Holloway kept his party some distance behind us, he having declined to join the consolidation of trains in order to avoid the inconvenience that the mingling of his stock with ours would entail, with reference to pasture, and camping facilities.

A mile or two behind Holloway were the trains of Captain Rountree, the Giles company, Simpson Fennell, Mr. Russell, and others, equipped with several wagons each, and accompanied by some loose stock.

All these were travelling along, a sort of moving neighbourhood; incidentally getting acquainted with one another, visiting on the road by day and in the camp at evening time; talking of the journey, of the country for which we were en route, and our hopes of prosperity and happiness in the new El Dorado—but most of all, just then, of the probable danger of attack by savage tribes.

More than ever rumours of impending trouble were flying from train to train. Some of these were to the effect that white bandits were in league with Indians in robbing and murdering emigrants. The well-known treachery of the savages, and the stories we heard of emigrants having been slaughtered also by whites—the real facts of which we knew little of—were quite enough to beget fear and suggest the need of plans for the best possible resistance.

Up to this time there was frequent communication between trains, a considerable distance ahead and behind. As at home, neighbour would visit neighbour, and discuss the topics of the day; so, from time to time we met persons in other trains who gave out information obtained before leaving home, or from mountaineers, trappers or explorers, occasionally met while we were yet on the eastern slope of the Rockies; men who were familiar with Indian dialects and at peace with the tribes, enabling them to learn much that was of importance to the emigrants.

Dissemination of news among the people of the various trains near us was accomplished not only during visits by members of one train to those of another, but sometimes by other methods. One of these, which was frequently employed in communicating generally or in signalling individuals known to be somewhere in the line behind us, was by a system of "*bone-writing*."

There were along the line of travel many bare, bleached bones of animals that had died in previous years, many of them doubtless the animals of earlier emigrants. Some of these, as for example, the frontal or the jaw-bone, whitened by the elements, and having some plain, smooth surface,

BONE-WRITING

were excellent tablets for pencil writing. An emigrant desiring to communicate with another, or with a company, to the rear, would write the message on one of these bones and place the relic on a heap of stones by the roadside, or suspend it in the branches of a sage bush, so conspicuously displayed that all coming after would see it and read. Those for general information, intended for all comers, were allowed to remain; others, after being read by the person addressed, were usually removed. Sometimes when passing such messages, placed by those ahead of us, we added postscripts to the bulletins, giving names and dates, for the edification of whomever might care to read them. It was in this way that some of the developments regarding the Indian situation were made known by one train to another.

Thus we progressed, counting off the average of about eighteen miles a day from the long part of the journey that still lay before us, when we reached Thousand Springs, adjacent to the present boundary line between Utah and Nevada. This, we were told, was the source of the Humboldt River. We were told, too, that the four hundred miles down the course of that peculiar stream—which we could not hope to traverse in much less than one month—we would find to be the most desert-like portion of the entire trip, the most disagreeable and arduous, for man and beast. Such was to be expected by reason of the character of that region and the greater danger there of Indian depredations; also because the passage through that section was to be undertaken after our teams had become greatly worn, therefore more likely to fail under hard conditions. Furthermore, scarcity of feed for the stock was predicted, and, along much of the way, uncertainty as to water supply, other than that from the Humboldt River, which was, especially at that time of the year, so strongly impregnated with alkali as to be dangerous to life.

Nearly all the face of the country was covered with alkali dust, which, in a light, pulverulent state, rose and filled the air at the slightest breeze or other disturbance. It was impossible to avoid inhaling this powder to some extent, and it created intense thirst, tending toward exhaustion and great suffering. We knew that sometimes delirium was induced by this cause, and even death resulted from it in cases of very long exposure under the worst conditions.

Sometimes for miles the only vegetable growth we found along the river was a string of willow bushes, fringing its course, and scattered, stunted sagebrush, growing feebly in gravel and dry sand, the leaves of which were partly withered and of a pale, ashy tint. Feed for the animals was very scarce. It was not possible, over much of the way, to get sufficient fresh water for the stock, therefore difficult to restrain them from drinking the river water. Some did drink from that stream, despite all efforts to prevent it, the result being that many of them died while we made our way along the sluggish Humboldt.

Chapter 5

The Holloway Massacre

It was decided that while in this region we would, whenever possible, make our camp some distance from the river, in order that the stock might be prevented from drinking the dangerous river water, also for the reason that the clumps of willows by the stream could be used as a cover by Indians bent on mischief: and they, we now believed, were watching for a favourable opportunity to surprise us.

It transpired that the Holloway party neglected this precaution, at least on one occasion, sometime after passing the head of the Humboldt River. Their train was next behind ours when, on the evening of August 13th, after rounding up their stock for the night, a short distance from the wagons, they stopped near the willows by the river and made what proved to be their last camp.

Behind them, but not within sight, were several emigrant camps at points varying from a few rods to half a mile apart.

The Holloway party retired as usual for the night; Mr. and Mrs. Holloway and their child, a girl of two years, in a small tent near the wagons; Jerry Bush, Mrs. Holloway's brother, and one of the hired men, Joe Blevens, in their blankets on the ground; while Bird Lawles, the other hired man, being ill with a fever, slept in a wagon.

There were others with this party that night; Mr. and Mrs.

Callum, Mr. Hattlebaugh, and a man whose name is now unknown. These four had been travelling near the Holloway party, and joined it for camping on that occasion.

The following morning Mr. Holloway was the first to arise. While making the camp-fire, he called to the others to get up, saying cheerfully:

"Well, we've got through one more night without a call from the Redskins."

"Bang, bang," rang out a volley of rifle shots, fired from the willows along the river, less than a hundred yards away.

Mr. Holloway fell, fatally shot, and died without a word or a struggle. As other members of the emigrant party sprang to their feet and came within view of the assailants, the firing continued, killing Joe Blevens, Mrs. Callum, and the man whose name is not recalled; while Bird Lawles, being discovered on his sick bed in a wagon, was instantly put to death.

Meanwhile Jerry Bush grasped his rifle and joined battle against the assassins. Thus far the savages remained hidden in the bushes, and Jerry's shots were fired merely at places where he saw the tall weeds and willows shaken by the motions of the Indians, therefore he has never known whether his bullets struck one of the enemy.

While thus fighting alone, for his life and that of his people, he received a gunshot in his side and fell. Knowing that he was unable to continue the fight, and, though doubting that he could rise, he endeavoured to shield himself from the bullets and arrows of the Indian band. He succeeded in dragging himself to the river bank, when, seizing a willow branch, he lowered himself to the foot of the steep cliff, some ten feet, reaching the water's edge. He then attempted to swim to the opposite shore. The effort caused him to lose his gun, in deep water. Owing to weakness due to his wound, he was unable to cross the stream.

Jerry Bush's parting view of the camp had revealed the apparent destruction of his entire party, except himself. Observing the body of at least one woman, among the victims on the ground, he believed that his sister also had been slain.

But Mrs. Holloway and the little girl were still in the tent, for the time unhurt, and just awakened from their morning slumber. Having realized that the camp was being attacked, Mrs. Holloway emerged from the tent to find no living member of her party in sight, other than herself and her child. For a moment she was partially shielded by the wagons. The first object that drew her attention was her husband's form, lying still in death, near the fire he had just kindled. Next beyond was the dead body of Blevens, and a little farther away were the remains of the others who had been slain. Her brother she did not see, but supposed he had met the same fate as the others whom she saw on the ground. Jerry was an experienced hunter; she knew that he always owned a fine gun, and had full confidence that, if he were alive and not disabled, he would defend his people to the last.

WITH HAND UPRAISED, IN SUPPLICATION, YIELDED TO THE IMPULSE TO FLEE

She saw some of the Indians coming from their ambush by the river. They approached for a time with caution, looking furtively about, as if to be sure there was no man left to defend the camp. As they drew nearer Mrs. Holloway realized that she and her child were facing an awful fate—death or captivity. On came the savages, now more boldly, and in greater numbers.

The terrified woman, clothed only in her night robe, barefooted; not knowing whether to take flight or stand and plead for mercy; with the child on one arm, one hand raised in supplication, yielded finally to the impulse to flee. As she started the attacking band resumed firing; she was struck, by arrows and at least one bullet, and dropped headlong to the ground.

Though conscious, she remained motionless, in the hope that, by feigning death she might escape further wounds and torture. But the Indians came, and taking the arrows from her body, punctured her flesh with the jagged instruments, as a test whether physical sensation would disclose a sign of life remaining. She lay with eyes closed; not a muscle twitched nor a finger moved, while those demons proceeded, in no delicate manner, to cut the skin around the head at the edge of the hair, then tear the scalp from the skull, leaving the bare and bleeding head on the ground.

Horrible as all this was, it did not prove to be the last nor the most revolting exhibition of wanton lust for blood.

The little girl, who it is hoped had been rendered insensible at sight of the cruelties perpetrated upon her mother, was taken by the feet and her brains dashed out on the wheels of a wagon. To this last act in the fiendish drama there was probably no witness other than the actors in it; but the child's body, mangled too terribly for description, and the bloody marks on the wagon, gave evidence so convincing that there could not be a moment's doubt of what had occurred.

The marauders now began a general looting of the wagons. Some of their number were rounding up the stock, preparing to drive the cattle away, when the trains of emigrants next in the rear appeared, less than half a mile distant. This caused the Indian band to retreat. They crossed the river, and then placing themselves behind the willows, hurried away, making their escape into the mountain fastnesses. Owing to their precipitous departure, much of the plunder they were preparing to take was left behind them. Among the articles thus dropped by them was the scalp of Mrs. Holloway, and the rescuing party found and took possession of it.

Those emigrants who first came upon the scene found Mrs. Holloway apparently dead; but, on taking her up, they saw that she was alive. Though returning to semi-consciousness some time later, her condition was such that she was unable to tell the story then; but there were evidences showing plainer than words could have told of the awful events of that morning, which had converted the quiet camp of this happy, hopeful company into a scene of death and destruction.

Before noon a large number of people of the great emigrant procession had arrived. They united in giving to the dead the best interment that the circumstances permitted. Then the broken and scattered effects of the Holloway company were gathered up, and the now mournful trains took position in the line of pilgrimage and again moved forward towards the Pacific.

Mr. Fennell, aided by Captain Rountree's company and others, attempted to save such of the Holloway property as had not been carried off or destroyed. They were successful in recovering about one hundred of the one hundred and fifty head of stock which the Indians had endeavoured to drive away. Two mules that were being led off by ropes

JERRY BUSH IN 1914

broke away from the savage band and returned, but the emigrants did not recover any of the stolen horses.

Jerry Bush found his way back to the scene. His injury, though apparently of a dangerous character, did not delay the relief parties more than a day after the attack, and the wound healed within a few weeks. It was reported that Callum and Hattlebaugh had escaped, but their further whereabouts was not known.

Captain Rountree took charge of Mrs. Holloway and her brother and brought them, with such of their stock and other belongings as remained, to The Meadows, on the Feather River. After partially recuperating there, an uncle, Mr. Perry Durban, came to their aid, and they were taken to Suisun. After full recovery from his wound, Jerry Bush located in Ukiah, and resided there some years. He still survives, now a resident of Hulett, Wyoming, at the ripe age of eighty years.

The slaughter of the Holloway party occurred at a point on the Humboldt River some thirty miles east of where Winnemucca is located, a few miles west of Battle Mountain. This becomes apparent by careful estimates of distance travelled per day, rather than by landmarks noted at the time, there being no settlements there, nor elsewhere along the route, at that time.

It was perhaps a year later when I went to a camp-meeting one Sunday, at Mark West Creek, in Sonoma County, California. The people attending a service were in a small opening among trees. Standing back of those who were seated, I saw among them a woman whose profile seemed familiar, and later I recognized her as Mrs. Holloway.

My interest in her career, due to her extraordinary part in the Indian massacre on the plains, was heightened by the fact that I had known her previously, as the daughter of Mr. Bush, a prosperous farmer, and had been present when she

Mrs. Nancy Holloway, 1857

married Mr. Holloway, in a little schoolhouse, near Rockport, Atchison County, Missouri. It seemed a natural impulse which prompted me to ask her for particulars of the tragedy, so disastrous to herself and her family; though later there were misgivings regarding the propriety of doing so.

Mrs. Holloway appeared at that time to be in good health, and was cheerful, possessing perfect control of her faculties. Her head was covered by a wig, made of her own hair, taken from the scalp that was recovered at the scene of the massacre.

All the heartrending experiences that she had endured were imprinted upon her mind in minutest detail, and she related them in the exact order of their occurrence. The recalling of the terrible ordeal, however, so wrought upon her emotions that she wept, to the limit of mild hysteria, which brought our conversation to a close, and soon thereafter she left the place.

I saw her no more; but learned sometime afterwards that her health failed, then of the giving away of her mental powers, and still later of her death, at Napa City; caused primarily by shock, and brooding over the misfortunes she had met on the bank of the Humboldt River.

It is difficult to believe that a woman, any woman—or any man—could, in a state of consciousness, endure such torture as was inflicted upon Mrs. Holloway, and refrain from disclosing to her tormentors that she was alive. But that she did so endure was her positive statement, and this was indisputably corroborated by evidences found by those who arrived at the scene less than an hour after the event.

Through the kindness of Mr. William Holloway, of Fairfax, Missouri, there is presented here a picture of Mrs. Nancy Holloway, wife of Smith Holloway. The photograph was taken in California, shortly after the attack described.

CHAPTER 6

Hope Sustains Patience

The appellation "Piker," much used in the West in early days, synonymous of "Missourian," had its origin on these plains. At first it was applied to a particular type of Missourian, but later came to be used generally.

There was among the emigrants a considerable number of persons from Pike County, Missouri. Some of these had the sign, "From Pike Co., Mo.," painted on their wagon covers. Others, when asked whence they came, promptly answered, "From Pike County, Missouri, by gosh, sir;" often said with a shrug implying that the speaker arrogated to himself much superiority by reason of the fact stated. The display of such signs, and announcements like that just mentioned, were of such frequent occurrence that the substance was soon abbreviated to "Piker," and became a by-word. It was often, perhaps always, spoken with a tinge of odium. Possibly this was due to the fact that many of the people referred to were of a "backwoods" class, rather short in culture, and in personal makeup, manner and language, bearing a general air of the extremely rural.

Though only persons of that description hailing from Pike County were those who at first had to bear the opprobrium generally implied by "Piker," later it was applied to all persons of that type in the Far West, regardless of their origin. Many years' of mingling of California's cosmopolitan population has changed all that; producing her present homogeneous, sterling, virile, and somewhat distinct type of "Californian"; so the "Piker," as such, is no longer in the land. A later application of the same word, descriptive of a person who does business in a small way, has nothing in common with the "Piker" of early days.

Fifty-eight years ago, the time of the events here narrated, was before the era of canned goods. Nearly all of the foodstuffs carried by the emigrants were in crude form, and bulky; but substantial, pure, and such as would keep in any climate.

During the first few weeks of the trip we milked some of the cows, and also made butter, the churning operation being effected mainly by the motion of the wagons, in the regular course. That this did not last long was due to reduction of milk supply. After a time there was not sufficient even for use in the coffee, or for making gravy, that convenient substitute for butter.

Such delicacies as may now be found in first-class canned meats, vegetables and milk would have filled an often-felt want. The occasional supply that we had en route of fresh meat and fish were obtained largely by chance; we having no knowledge of localities where hunting and fishing were likely to be successful, and it being deemed unsafe for members of the party to wander far or remain long away from the train. It seems regrettable that the invention of hermetically-sealed and easily portable foods, and the inducement to cross the plains to California, did not occur in reversed sequence.

Neither had the Kodak arrived. Had it been with us then, this narrative might be illustrated with snap-shots of camp scenes, characteristic roadside views, and incidents of travel generally, which would do more for realism than can any word-picture. We often see specimens of artists' work purporting to represent a "'49er" emigrant train on the overland journey—some of them very clever; but seldom are they at all realistic to the man who was there.

The man with a camera could have perpetuated, for example, the striking scene presented to us one day of a party, consisting of two men and their wives, with two or three children, sitting on a rocky hillside, woefully scanning their team of done-out oxen and one wagon with a broken axle; no means at hand for recuperation and repair. In the scorching sun of a July day they waited, utterly helpless, hopeless, forlorn, confused; and a thousand miles from "anywhere." Such a grouping would not have made a cheerful picture, but would have assisted immensely in recording a historical fact.

But no emigrant ever found another in distress and "passed by on the other side."

We were early risers, and the camp was each morning a scene of life with the rising of the sun. By sunset all were sufficiently fatigued to wish for making camp again. Therefore, from the morning start till the evening stop was usually about twelve hours, with variations from time to time, according to necessity or exceptional conditions. Breaking camp in the morning became routine, and proceeded like clockwork. Each patient ox voluntarily drew near, and stood, waiting to be yoked with his fellow and chained to his daily task. So well did each know his place by the side of his mate that the driver had only to place one end of the yoke on the neck of the "off" ox, known, for example, as "Bright," and hold the other end toward the "nigh" ox, saying, "Come under here, Buck," and the obedient fellow placed himself in position. Then the bows were placed and keyed, and "Bright" and "Buck" were hitched for duty. It required but a few minutes to put three or four yoke of oxen in working order.

As the result of much repetition, the packing of the camp articles onto the wagons was done dexterously and quickly. Each box, roll and bundle had a designated place; all being arranged usually to facilitate sitting or reclining positions for those who rode in the "schooners," that they might be as comfortable as possible, and read, sleep, or, as the women often did, sew and knit, or play games. During some parts of the trip such means of whiling away the hours was very desirable, if not a necessity. If there ever was a time or condition in which it could be pardonable to "kill time," these circumstances were there, during many long days.

The bivouac was always a scene of bustle and orderly disorder, especially if the camp-site was a good one: wood, water and grass being the desiderata. Obedient to habit, every person and animal dropped into place and action. With the wagons drawn to position for the night's sojourn, teams were quickly unhitched, the yokes, chains, harness and saddles falling to the ground where the animals stood.

Relieved of their trappings, the oxen, horses and mules were turned to pasture, plentiful or scant. Cooking utensils came rattling from boxes; rolls of bedding tumbled out and were spread on the smoothest spots of sand or grass. Eager hands gathered such fuel as was available, and the camp-fire blazed. Buckets of water were brought from the spring or stream; and in an incredibly short time the scene of animation had wrought full preparation for the night, while the odour of steaming coffee and frying bacon rendered the astonished air redolent of appetizing cookery.

Some families used a folding table, on which to serve meals; but more spread an oilcloth on the ground and gathered around that; or individuals, taking a plate and a portion, sat on a wagon-tongue or a convenient stone. Camp-stools and "split-bottomed" chairs were among the luxuries that some carried, in limited numbers; but these were not useful especially as seats while partaking of a meal spread on the ground.

Appetites were seldom at fault; and the meals, though plain and of little variety, were never slighted. It is hardly necessary to add that bacon and coffee were easy staples. Bread was mainly in the form of quick-fire biscuits, baked in a skillet or similar utensil, or the ever-ready and always-welcome "flap-jack," sometimes supplemented with soda-crackers, as a delicacy.

Nearly all the nights were pleasant—mild temperature, and very little dew. This gave much relief, the daytime heat being generally irksome and often distressingly hot. Many of the men came to prefer sleeping wholly in the open, with the heavens unobscured; often requiring no more than a pair of blankets and a small pillow.

Early evening was devoted to social gatherings. If the night was pleasant groups would assemble, for conversation, singing and story-telling; varied with dancing by the young people of some companies. The more religious sang hymns and read the Bible sometimes, in lieu of attendance at any church service. When wood was plentiful, a bonfire added to the cheerfulness and comfort of the occasion. Often neighbouring trains camped quite near, when much enjoyment was found in visits by the members of one company among those of another. In such ways many agreeable acquaintances were met and even lasting friendships formed, some of which have endured throughout the nearly three-score years since passed.

But we were not always favoured with clear and pleasant weather. No one who was there can have forgotten one night at the Platte River, when we had a most dismal experience. Rain began falling in the afternoon, and for that reason we made camp early.

The tents were set up on a bit of flat ground near the river bank. There were some large trees, but little dry wood available for fuel for the camp fire except on an island, which was separated from us by a branch of the river, about twenty yards wide and a foot deep. Some of us waded over, getting our clothes soaked; others crossed on horseback, and carried back from the island enough wood to make a fire. But, time after time, the fire was quenched by the rain, which now was falling in torrents; so we had much difficulty in preparing our supper.

The people huddled into the tents and wagons, half hungry, more than half wet, and uncomfortable altogether. With the exception of one or two cots, the bedding was spread on the ground in the tents, and all turned in—but not for long. Some one said, "water is running under my bed." Then another and another made the same complaint. Soon we learned the deplorable fact that the large tent had been pitched in a basin-like place, and that the water, as the rain increased, was coming in from all sides, the volume growing rapidly greater.

We succeeded then in lighting one lantern, when the water was found to be something like two inches deep over nearly all parts of the large tent's floor. The beds were taken up and placed in soaked heaps, on camp stools and boxes; and the rain continued pouring in steady, relentless disregard of our misery. Except where lighted by the single lantern the darkness was, of course, absolute. Relief was impossible. There appearing to be nothing else to do, everybody abandoned the tents and huddled in the wagons; the lantern was blown out, and there was little sleep, while we waited and wished for daylight.

Some of the days were warm and some hot. Some were very hot. Discomforts were common; and yet not much was said, and apparently little thought, of them. Having become inured to the conditions as we found them from time to time, discomforts, such as under other circumstances would have been considered intolerable, were passed without comment. There were times and situations in which hardships were unavoidable, some of them almost unendurable; but these, having been anticipated, were perhaps less poignant in the enduring than in the expectation.

Let us for a moment raise the curtain of more than half a century, while we look back on one of those ox-drawn trains of "prairie-schooners," as it appeared to an observer on the ground at the time; about the middle of August, and beyond the middle of the journey. Permit the imagination to place the scene alongside that of the present-day modes of traversing the same territory, when the distance is covered in a less number of days than it required of months then. Perhaps such a comparison may help to form some faint conception of what the overland pioneers did, and what they felt, and saw, and were.

There they are as we see them, on a long stretch of sage-brush plateau. The surface of the plain is only sand and gravel, as far as the eye can reach. The atmosphere is hazy, with dust and vibrating waves of heat arising from the ground. Far away to the northwest is the outline of some mountains, just visible in the dim distance. In the opposite direction, whence we have come, there is nothing above the ground but hot space, and dust. Not a living thing in sight but ourselves and ours.

The animals appear fatigued, jaded. The people appear— well, as to physical condition, like the animals: generally all look alike. Yet the people seem hopeful. And why hopeful? The inherent and indomitable trait of the race which makes it possible for humanity to look over and past present difficulties, however great, and see some good beyond. That is why the world "do move." Often, as it was with us, progress may be slow, but every day counts for a little.

Just here twelve or fifteen miles a day is doing well—very well. From a slight eminence at one side of the way we may stand and see the slowly creeping line of wagons and stock, for many miles fore and aft, as they bend their way in and out, around and over the surface of knolls and flats, hillocks and gullies. From a distant view they seem not to be moving at all.

The hour of mid-day arrives, and they stop for the "nooning." There is nothing growing in the vicinity that the horses and cattle can eat, and no water except the little in the keg and canteens; so the carrying animals stand in their yokes and harness, or under saddles, and the loose stock wait in groups, their thirst unslaked.

As the people come out of the wagons and go about the business of the hour we see the marks of the elements upon them. The women wear "poke" bonnets and gingham dresses. The men are unshaven. All are sunburnt to a rich, leathern brown. Some are thin, and at this particular time, wearing a serious expression. They are not as unhappy as they look, their principal trouble of the moment being merely anxiety to satisfy prodigious and healthy appetites.

There, under the stress of the midsummer sun, now in the zenith, no shade, no protection from the flying dust, they proceed cheerfully to build a fire, of sticks and dry weeds; they fry bacon and bake biscuits, prepare large pots of coffee, and they eat, from tin plates, and drink from tin cups.

No one says, "This is awful!" They laugh as they eat, saying, "Good; ain't it?"

This is not a cheerful view altogether of the retrospective; but a sketch true to life, as life was there. It was not all like that. A good deal of it was.

Some will say that these overland travellers were overzealous, even foolhardy. One of the earliest pioneers, Mr. Daniel B. Miller, who reached Oregon by the plains route in 1852, wrote later to relatives in Illinois, "I would not bring a family across for all that is contained in Oregon and California." Himself single, he had come with a train composed almost wholly of men, but learned incidentally what risks there were in escorting women and children through the wilds.

But the enduring of all this toil, exposure and hardship had for its inspiration the buoyant hope of something good just beyond, something that was believed to be worthy of the privation and effort it was costing. The ardour of that hope was too intense to be discouraged by anything that human strength could overcome. The memories of those strenuous experiences are held as all but sacred, and you never meet one of these early overland emigrants who does not like to sit by your fireside and tell you about it. He forgets, for the moment, how hard it was, and dwells upon it, telling it over and over again, with the same pride and sense of noble achievement that the old soldier feels when recounting the battles and the camp life and the hard marches of the war, when he was young, away back in the sixties. One crossing this country by present-day conveyances, in richly appointed railroad trains, with all the comforts obtainable in modern sleeping, dining and parlour cars, can hardly be expected to conceive what it was to cover the same course under the conditions described; when there was not even a poor wagon road, and the utmost speed did not equal in a day the distance travelled in half an hour by the present mode. Any person who rides in a cumbrous and heavily laden wagon, behind a team whose pace never exceeds a slow walk; over dusty ground, in hot weather, will, before one day is passed, feel that endurance requires utmost fortitude. Consider what patience must be his if the journey continues for four, five or six long months!

It is worthy of mention that there was no dissension among our people, nor even unpleasantness, during the entire trip, nor did we observe any among others. We were fortunate in having no "grouches" among us. Harmony, cheerfulness, a disposition to be jolly, even to the degree of hilarity, was the prevailing spirit. That, too, under circumstances often so trying that they might have thrown a sensitive disposition out of balance. All this in the wilds of an unorganized territory, where there was no law to govern, other than the character and natural bent of individuals. Such lack of established authority we had thought might lead to recklessness or aggressive conduct, but it did not.

Present residents in the fields and valleys, and the prosperous towns along much of the line of travel described, will find it difficult to reconcile the accounts here given with conditions as they see them now. Leagues of territory now bearing a network of railroads and splendid highways, which carry rich harvests from the well-tilled farms, and connect numerous cities, was thought of ordinarily by the emigrants in early days only as it appeared to them, and then was, the stamping ground of savage tribes and the home of wild beasts, untouched by the transforming hand of civilization. To the keen observer, however, it was evident that we were passing through a great deal of fine country. On the other hand, it cannot be denied that part of that journey was through lands naturally barren, some desert wastes, much of which is still unreclaimed, some unreclaimable.

CHAPTER 7

Tangled by a Tornado

Few readers need peruse these pages to learn what a thunder-storm is like, but many may not know what it is to encounter a fierce electrical disturbance while surrounded by a herd of uncontrollable cattle on the prairie.

On an occasion after having stopped for a "nooning," there loomed up suddenly in the northwest a black, ominous cloud, revolving swiftly and threateningly, as might the vapours from some gigantic cauldron; variegated in black, blue and green, bespangled with red streaks of lightning.

This display of the angry elements was making a broadening sweep onward directly towards where we were. The air turned black and murky, and was vibrant with electric tension. Flocks of buzzards flew low to the earth about us, as if to be ready for the carrion of the impending catastrophe. The fear instinct of the brute seized the cattle, and they hovered together, bellowing, distraught with apprehension of evil.

The whirlpool of atmospheric chaos grew more intense and rapidly larger as it approached. Globules of water began to "spat! spat!" on the ground, here and there, as the storm-cloud opened its batteries of liquid balls. There was only such protection as the wagons afforded. Whatever preparation we could make must be effected at once.

Knowing that if the cattle should take fright and run, it would be better that they leave the wagons, I dropped the wagon-tongue to which I was hitching a team, and called to a boy who was hooking up the next wagon, telling him not to do so. He had, however, already attached to that wagon the team consisting of three yoke of oxen.

The big drops of water were in a moment followed by hailstones, at first very large and scattering, striking the ground each with a vicious thud—a subdued "whack"; growing more frequent and presently mingled with lesser ones; until, in the shortest moment, there was a cloud-burst of hail and rain pouring upon us, a storm such as none of us had ever witnessed.

The oxen, chained together in strings of three and four pairs, pelted by the hail, were mutinous and altogether uncontrollable. My own string, having turned crosswise of the front end of the wagon, were pushing it backward, down the hillside. The team in charge of the boy, being attached to their wagon and heading away from the storm, were turning the wagon over. Knowing that the boy's mother was in the "schooner," on a sick bed, I left my wagon and ran to that. As the oxen, in trying to shield themselves from the hail, were forcing the front wheels around under the wagon-box, I was fortunate enough to get a shoulder under one corner of the box and exert sufficient force to prevent the wagon upsetting. All this took little more than a minute. The storm passed away as suddenly as it had come. Then I saw the wagon which was my special charge lying on its side, at the bottom of the slope; the bows of the cover fitting snugly into a sort of natural gutter, with a swift current of muddy water and hailstones flowing through the cover, as if it were a sluice-pipe. Everything in the wagon was topsy-turvy; and, half buried in the heap were two little girls, who had been riding in the vehicle. They were

THE AUTHOR—TWENTY YEARS AFTER

more frightened than hurt, but complained loudly at being placed in a cold-storage of hailstones.

Meantime, the sun beamed again, clear and hot, and we saw the storm-cloud pursuing its course over the plain to the southeast, leaving in its wake a wet path a few rods wide.

The other men had their hands full in caring for endangered members of the party and the equipment. The loose stock had stampeded and were far away, with some of the mounted men in desperate pursuit. They eventually brought the cattle to a halt, about five miles away, where the wagons overtook them when it was time to make camp.

Continuous travel over rough ground and through deep sand, and ascending steep mountains, proved too great a strain for the endurance of some outfits. From time to time we were obliged to witness instances of extreme privation and hardship, usually the result of inadequate preparation for the arduous journey. Some started with only enough oxen to carry them in case all should remain serviceable; and carried provisions for no more than the shortest limit of time estimated; so that the mishap of losing an ox or two, or any delay, worked a calamity. Some trains started so late, or were so much delayed, that they were compelled to negotiate passage of the higher mountains after the time when enormous snow-drifts had to be encountered; further delay resulting, with exhaustion of strength and depletion of supplies, in consequence of which many members of some trains failed to reach their destination. A notable experience of this kind was that of the Donner party, in 1846.

It was in one of the higher mountain regions that we overtook one Eben Darby and his family. Darby had been with one of the trains in advance of us, but being unable to keep the pace, he was obliged to fall behind. He had one small wagon, two yoke of oxen, and a cow; the latter led by a rope behind the wagon. His wife, with a young baby, and the wife's brother, Danny Worley, were the only persons with Darby. The wife was a weak, inexperienced girl; the child sickly. Mrs. Darby's brother was a large, fat youth of nineteen, whose distinguishing and inconvenient characteristic was an abnormal appetite. Their provisions were nearly exhausted. The cow was to them the real fountain of life. She was doing nobly—supplying them a quart of milk a day, which was wonderful, considering the circumstances. This milk fed the baby, and afforded a good substitute for butter, in the form of milk gravy—on which Danny fared sumptuously every day.

Later their oxen drank of the alkali water of the Humboldt River, and three of the four died in one night. Then the cow was yoked with the remaining ox, two steers were loaned them by "good Samaritans" in our company, and they were with us to the Sink of the Humboldt.

Meantime the milk supply grew less, and Mrs. Darby was compelled to substitute water for milk in the gravy. This sop was not satisfactory to Danny. One evening at meal time he was overheard by some of our boys, saying, "I want milk in my gravy." Though reminded there was only enough milk for the baby, he of the phenomenal appetite reiterated, "I don't care, I want milk in my gravy." Thereafter "Gravy" was the name by which he was known, so long as he travelled with us.

This narrative would not do justice to the variety of individuals and events without mention of another singular personage, a young fellow who was "working his passage"; a sort of disconnected unit, whose place became everywhere in the train, and who belonged to nobody. How he got smuggled into the company no one has since been able to recall. He was a sort of desert stowaway; tolerated because, though eccentric and quite alarming in appearance, he was always in good humour, and often useful, having a willingness to do as many of the chores as others would trust him to perform. He was notable as a physical curiosity, though not actually deformed. Low of stature, he came to be known as "Shorty," the only name we ever had for him. As he stood, his abnormally long arms enabled him to take his hat from the ground without stooping. His legs were not mates in length, causing him as he moved, with a quick, rocking gait, to create the impression that he might topple backward; but somehow the longer leg always got underneath at the critical instant, and restored the balance. His head was large, and perfectly round; hair porcupinesque, each bristle standing nearly perpendicular to the plane on which it grew. He had no neck. Mouth small, and so round that it opened not unlike a bored hole in a flesh-coloured pumpkin.

"Shorty" asserted that he was a singer. He and "Jack" never sang together, however—that is, they never did so any more, after trying it once. "Shorty" and "Gravy" Worley became chums inseparable, except on one occasion, when their friendship was temporarily ruptured by a dispute over the ownership of a fishing hook. Anger grew hot, but when they were about to come to blows, "Shorty" suddenly dropped on "all-fours" and essayed to butt his adversary with his head, which surprising mode of combat so disconcerted "Gravy" that he ran for his quarters, wildly yelling, "Take him off, take him off."

For a time during the early part of the journey the horses and mules were picketed at night, on the best pasture available; and before we retired, all the animals were brought near the wagons, the loose cattle bunched with them, and guards were placed, to prevent straying of the stock or surprise by Indians. Later, for awhile, these precautions were deemed unnecessary, though still later they had to be resumed. The stock became accustomed to the daily routine, and after the all-day travel, were quite willing, when they had finished their evening grazing, to assemble near the camp and lie down for the night, usually remaining comparatively quiet till morning. As if having some realization of the lonely nature of the surroundings, the animals were not disposed to stray off, except on rare occasions; but rather to keep within sight of the people and the wagons.

There was proof of the theory that in some circumstances domestic animals acquire some of that feeling that human creatures know, when far from the habitations of man. There is a peculiar sensation in the great and boundless contiguity of empty silence which works the senses up to a feeling that is somewhat alike in man and beast—that there is most comfort and protection near the centre of the settlement or camp. In this stillness of the night—and night on these plains was often very still—any slight noise outside the camp startled and thrilled the taut nerves. Not only was the night still; usually it was silent, too.

But occasionally, when the silence was absolute, a couple or more of prairie-wolves lurking in the vicinity, without the faintest note of prelude, would startle the calm of night with their peculiar commingling of barks, howls and wails,—a racket all their own. It was the habit of these night prowlers of the desert to come as near to the camp as their acute sense of safety permitted, and there, sitting on their haunches, their noses pointed to the moon, render a serenade that was truly thrilling. Two prairie-wolves, in a fugued duet, can emit more disquieting noise, with a less proportion of harmony, than any aggregation of several times their equal in numbers, not excepting Indians on the war-path or a "gutter" band.

That awe of the wilderness to which reference has been made, and its effect on the nerves, may explain the stampede of cattle, often not otherwise accounted for; which occurs sometimes in these hollow solitudes. It occurs nowhere else that I have known.

Several times we experienced this strange exhibition of sudden panic; the snapping, as it were, of the nerves, from undue tension, when, instantly, from cause then to us unknown and unguessed, the whole band of cattle, teams as well as loose stock, made a sudden, wild, furious dash, in a compact mass; seeming instinctively to follow in whatever direction the leader's impulse led him; drifting together and forward as naturally as water flows to the current; with heads and tails high in air; blindly trampling to the earth whatever chanced to be in their path.

These were not in any sense wild stock. The cattle, horses and mules were all animals that had been raised on the quiet farms of the Middle West, well domesticated.

In the light of certain modern theories it might be said by some that these otherwise docile animals stampeded on the unpeopled plains because they heard the "call of the wild." There were, however, occasions when the cause could be readily assigned for this temporary casting off of restraint.

A COYOTE SERENADE

In one instance, already mentioned, a sudden, pelting hailstorm was the undoubted cause; when, taking the stampede temper, they ran five or six miles before the man, mounted on one of our fleetest saddle-horses, got in front of the foremost of them and checked their running.

On all such occasions control could be regained in only one way. Speeding his horse till he overtook and passed the leader of the drove the rider made his horse the leader; and as each loose animal always followed whatever was in front, the horseman, by making a circuit and gradually slackening the pace, led the drove around and back to place in the line of travel.

Naturally one source of uneasiness was the thought of what our situation would be if, on one of these occasions, we should fail to regain control of these animals, so necessary to us in continuing the westward journey. A stampede when some of the oxen were yoked to the wagons was, of course, more serious in its immediate consequences than when it happened while all were detached from the equipment.

A stampede occurred one day in a level stretch of country, open in every direction; nothing in sight to cause alarm. There the emigrant road showed plainly before us. The wagons were in open single file, the loose stock drawn out in line at the rear. Men on horseback, hats over their eyes, some of them with one leg curled over the pommel of the saddle; lazily droning away the slow hours and the humdrum miles. The women and children were stowed away on bundles of baggage and camp stuff in the wagons, some of them asleep perhaps, rocked in their "schooner" cradles. A few of the men and boys perchance were strolling off the way, in the hope of starting a sage grouse or rabbit from some sheltering clump of brush. During a specially quiet routine like this; the cattle lolling behind the wagons, mostly unattended, keeping the snail pace set by the patient teams;

a steer now and again turning aside to appropriate a tuft of bunch-grass; their white horns rising and falling in the brilliant sunlight, with the swaying motion of their bodies as they walked, shimmered like waves of a lake at noonday before a gentle breeze: quickly as a clap of the hands, every loose beast in the band, in the wildest fashion of terror, started, straight in the course of the moving line—pell-mell, they went, veering for nothing that they could run over; sweeping on, with a roaring tramp, like muffled thunder, they passed along both sides of the train. The teams, catching the frenzy, took up the race, as best they could with their heavy impedimenta; all beyond control of their drivers or the herders, who, startled from the reverie of the moment, could do no better than dodge to such place of safety as they found, and stand aghast at the spectacle. Fortunately the draft oxen usually were forced to stop running before they went far, owing to the weight of the wagons they hauled and their inability to break the yokes.

In this particular instance the most serious casualty was the death of a boy, about eight years of age, the son of Dr. Kidd. The child was probably asleep in a wagon, and being aroused by the unusual commotion, may have attempted to look out, when a jolt of the wagon threw him to the ground, and he was trampled to death. The body was kept in camp overnight, and the next morning wrapped in a sheet and buried by the roadside.

This was in a vast stretch of lonely plain. As we journeyed through it, viewing the trackless hills and rock-ribbed mountains not far away on either side, mostly barren and uninviting, it was difficult to conceive of that territory ever becoming the permanent homes of men. Yet it is possible, and probable, that the grave of Dr. Kidd's little boy is today within the limits of a populous community, or even beneath a noisy thoroughfare of some busy town.

Chapter 8

Disaster

Our consolidated train continued its creeping pace down the meandering Humboldt; crossing the stream occasionally, to gain the advantage of a shorter or better road.

Soon again there were other proofs of the wisdom we had shown in taking every possible precaution against attack.

Next ahead of us was a family from England, a Mr. Wood, his wife and one child, with two men employed as drivers. They were outfitted with three vehicles, two of them drawn by ox teams, in charge of the hired men, and a lighter, spring-wagon, drawn by four mules, the family conveyance, driven by Mr. Wood. We had not known them before.

One very hot day in the latter part of August, after having moved along for a time with no train in sight ahead of us, we came upon Mr. Wood in a most pitiable plight, the result of an attack and slaughter, not differing greatly from the Holloway case, and its parallel in atrocity.

Mr. Wood's party had spent the preceding night undisturbed, and were up early in the morning, preparing to resume their journey. The ox teams had been made ready and moved on, while Mr. Wood proceeded in a leisurely way with harnessing the four mules and attaching them to the smaller wagon. All the articles of their equipment had been gathered up and placed in proper order in the wagon.

When Mr. Wood had nearly completed hitching the team, Mrs. Wood and the baby being already in the wagon, some men, apparently all Indians, twenty or more of them, were seen coming on horseback, galloping rapidly from the hills to the northward, about half a mile away.

Mr. Wood, fearing that he and his family were about to be attacked, in this lonely situation, hurriedly sprang to the wagon seat and whipped up the mules, hoping that before the attack they could come within sight of the ox wagons, which had rounded the point of a hill but a few minutes before, and have such aid as his hired men could give.

He had no more than got the team under way when a wheel came off the wagon—he having probably over-looked replacing the nut after oiling the axle. Notwith-standing this he lost no time in making the best of the circumstances. Jumping to the ground, he hurriedly placed Mrs. Wood on one of the mules, cutting the harness to re-lease the animal from the wagon; then, with the baby in his arms, he mounted another mule, and they started flight.

But the Indians had by this time come within gun-shot range and fired upon them. Mrs. Wood fell from the mule, fatally shot. Mr. Wood's mule was shot under him, and dropped; next Mr. Wood received a bullet in the right arm, that opened the flesh from wrist to elbow. That or another shot killed the child. Amidst a shower of bullets, Mr. Wood ran in the direction taken by his ox wagons. Getting past the point of the low hill that lay just before him without being struck again, he was then beyond range of the firing, and soon overtook his wagons. His men, with all the guns they had, returned, to find the woman and child dead on the ground. One of the mules was dead, one wounded, the other two gone. The wagon had been ransacked of its con-tents, and the band of assassins were making their way back into the hills whence they had come.

This small wagon, Mr. Wood said, had contained the family effects; and among them were several articles of considerable value, all of which had been taken. Among his property were pieces of English gold coin, the equivalent of fifteen hundred dollars. It had been concealed in the bottom of the wagon-box, and he had supposed the band would overlook it; but that, too, was gone.

Such was the plight in which our company found the man, soon after this tragedy was so swiftly enacted, and which so effectually bereft him of all, his family and his property, leaving him wounded, and dependent on the mercy of strangers.

The dead were placed in mummy-form wrappings and buried, mother and child in one, unmarked grave.

When the manuscript of this narrative was first made ready for the printer, the description of the calamity which befell Mr. Wood and his family ended here. There were other details, as clearly recalled as those already recited, but so atrocious and devoid of motive, that it was a matter of grave doubt whether the facts should be given. It seemed too deplorable that such an occurrence could be recorded as the act of human beings; furthermore, would it be credible? It has been intimated that the present endeavour is to give a complete history of events as they occurred: no material item suppressed, nothing imaginary included; therefore the remaining details are given.

Incredible as it may sound to civilized ears, after the bodies of Mrs. Wood and her child had been interred, hardly had those who performed this service gone from the spot when a part of the savage band that had murdered those innocent victims, rushed wildly back to the place, disinterred the bodies from the shallow grave, taking the sheets in which the bodies had been wrapped, and which were their only covering, and carrying those articles away. When the Indians had gone a second time, the grief-stricken Mr. Wood returned and reinterred the remains of his wife and child.

Mr. Wood's wounded arm was dressed by Dr. Maxwell and Dr. Kidd, his wagons were placed in the lead of our train, and again we moved westward.

CHAPTER 9

Mysterious Visitors

The next following day, as we wended our way among the sand dunes, alkali flats and faded sagebrush, there came to us—whence we knew not—three men, equipped with a small wagon, covered with white ducking, arched over bows, similar to the covering on most of the emigrant wagons; drawn by two large, handsome, well-harnessed horses; all having a well-to-do appearance, that made our dusty, travel-worn outfits look very cheap and inferior.

They told us that they were mountaineers, of long experience on the plains; well acquainted with the Indians and familiar with their habits and savage proclivities. They said that the Shoshone Indians were very angry at the white people who were passing through their lands; that this hostility recently had been further aroused by certain alleged acts of the whites along the emigrant road; and that the feeling was now so intense that even they, our informants, were alarmed, notwithstanding their long, intimate and friendly intercourse with these Indians; and, believing themselves no longer safe among the tribe, they were anxious to get out of the Shoshone country; therefore they requested the privilege of placing themselves under the protection of our large train until we should have passed out of the Shoshone lands and into those of the Pah-Utes, which tribe they said was known to be friendly toward the white race.

One of these men was a specially picturesque figure; weighty, with large, square shoulders; well-formed head; full, brown beard, cropped short. He wore a deer-skin blouse, leathern breeches; broad, stiff-brimmed hat, low crown, flat top, decorated with a tasselled leather band; a fully-loaded ammunition belt—a combination make-up of cowboy, mountaineer and highwayman.

The three men spoke plain English, with a free use of "frontier adjectives."

Having received permission to take temporary protection by travelling near us, they placed themselves at the rear of our train, and that night pitched camp slightly apart from our circle of wagons.

Some of our men visited them during the evening, eager to hear their tales of adventure; and listened, open-mouthed, to descriptions of life among savage associations, in the mountain wilds, jungles and the desert plains.

The visitors dwelt with emphasis on the threatening attitude of the Shoshone Indians towards the emigrants; warning us that our position was hazardous, with caution that there was special risk incurred by individuals who wandered away from the train, thus inviting a chance of being shot by Redskins, ambushed among the bunches of sagebrush. They were especially earnest as they assured us of the peril there would be in loitering away from the body of the company, as they had noticed some of our boys doing, that day, while hunting for sage fowls.

After awhile, he of the big hat inquired—and seemed almost to tremble with solicitude as he spoke:

"Are you prepared to defend yourselves, in case of an attack?"

Here unpleasant surmises gave place to distinct suspicions in the minds of some of our older men. They regarded that question as a "Give-away." All the day, since these three joined us, we had felt that they might be spies, and in league with the Indians. So now not a few of us were giving closest attention, both with ears and eyes.

An answer was ready: That we were prepared, and waiting for the encounter; with a hundred and twenty-five shots for the first round; that we could reload as rapidly as could the Indians; and had ammunition in store for a long siege.

The actual fact was that, although every man of us had some sort of a "shooting-iron," they were not formidable. In kind, these varied well through the entire range of infantry, from a four-inch six-shooter to a four-foot muzzle-loader, and from a single-barrelled shotgun on up to a Sharp's repeating rifle. The weapon last mentioned carried a rotating cylinder, for five shells, and was the latest thing in quick-fire repeating arms of that time: but there was only one of that class in the train. Had we been seen on muster, standing at "present arms," the array would have been less terrifying than comical.

Just how our visitors received our bluff with reference to preparedness for battle we could not know. The next morning these mysterious strangers took position in the rear of our train once more, carrying a small white flag, mounted on a pole fastened to their wagon. Upon being asked the purpose of the flag they replied that it served as a signal to any one of their number who might go beyond view, enabling him to determine the location of the wagon.

Captain John reminded them that, according to their statements, wandering out of sight was too hazardous to be done or considered; adding that therefore there did not seem to be any need of the flag, and he wanted it to be taken down.

It came down.

During the noon-hour stop that day, while the doctors were dressing Mr. Wood's wounded arm, he obtained a first look at our three protégés. He at once indicated the man wearing the big, brown hat, and stated, excitedly but confidentially, to those of our company who were near him:

"I believe that man was with the Indians who killed my wife and child."

That statement naturally created a much greater feeling of uneasiness among us. The assertion was whispered around; and every man of us became a detective. The leading men of our party put their heads together in council. The situation was more than ever grave and the suspense distinctly painful. We feared something tragic would happen any hour.

Mr. Wood was asked to obtain another view of the man and endeavour to make his statement more definite, if he could. His wound, and the terrible shock he had sustained two days previously, had so prostrated him that he was unable to make haste. Arrangements were made to disguise him and have him go where he could obtain a good view of the three men, but his condition prevented it.

Later in the afternoon the three-men-afraid-of-Indians announced that we had passed out of the territory of the savage Shoshones; they felt it would be safe for them to dispense with our kind escort, therefore, after camping near us that night, they would withdraw and bid us a thankful goodbye.

We camped that night on a level place, where there was sage-brush three or four feet high, and thick enough to make good cover for an enemy. Our people, having become thoroughly distrustful of the three men who had made themselves appendages of our train, feared an attack would be made on our camp that night. Suspicion had developed into a fixed belief that the trio were confederates of the Shoshones, and had come to us under a pretence of fear on their part, in order to spy out the fighting strength of our company.

The place where they halted their wagon and prepared to spend the night was not more than a hundred yards from where our vehicles were arranged, in the usual hollow circle, with the camp-fire and the people enclosed.

When darkness set in, guards of our best men, armed with the most effective guns we had, were quietly distributed about the camp, the chosen men crawling on their hands and knees to their allotted positions, in order that the three strangers should not know our arrangements. There was an understanding that, if there should be an attack during the night, the first thing to do was, if possible, to shoot those three men; for, under the circumstances, any attack occurring that night would be deemed completion of proof that they were responsible for it and for any atrocity that might follow or be attempted.

The night passed without notable happening—except that at the break of day the three men and their wagon silently stole away.

There was a feeling of great relief on being rid of them; but there remained some apprehension of their turning up at some unguarded moment and unpleasant place, to make us trouble; for their absence did not remove the impression that they had come among us to gauge our desirability as prey and the feasibility of overpowering our entire train.

CHAPTER 10

Challenge to Battle

We divided our long train into two parts, leaving a short space between the sections. Mr. Wood's two wagons headed the forward part. Toward the close of the day on which this change of arrangement was made, the forward section turned off the road a short distance before stopping to make camp, and the rear section passed slightly beyond the first, left the road and halted, so that a double camp was formed, with the two sections thus placed for the night in relative positions the reverse of the order they had maintained during the day.

At night-fall, when supper was over and everything at rest, we saw three horsemen going westward on the emigrant road. When they were opposite the Maxwell, or forward, camp, as the train sections had been placed, these men turned from the road and came toward us. We soon recognized them as our late guests on the way: he of the big hat and his two companions.

Riding into our camp, one of them remarked that they now observed the change made in arrangement of our train, explaining that they had intended to call on the Englishman, whose place had been in the lead. They apologized for their mistake. The first speaker added that they had heard it stated that this English gentleman had charged one of their number with being in company with the Indians who killed his wife, at the time of the tragedy, a few days before.

He of the big, brown hat then assumed the role of spokesman, and said:

"I understand that he indicated me, by description; and if that man says I was with the Indians who killed his wife, I will kill him. Let him say it, and I will shoot him down like a dog, that he is. I am here to demand of him if he said it."

Another of the three said, in a tone of conciliation:

"We are honest men. We came out here from Stockton, California, where we live, to meet the emigrants as they come over from the States. We buy their weak and disabled stock, such as cannot finish the trip to the Coast; take the animals onto range that we know of, and in the fall, when they are recuperated, we drive them in for the California market."

The man under the large hat resumed:

"My name is James Tooly. My partners here, are two brothers, named Hawes. And now, if that Englishman, or any one among you, says I was with the Indians who killed his wife, I will shoot him who says it, right here before you all."

This was said with much vehemence, and punctuated with many oaths.

Mr. Drennan, of our combined company, replied:

"If you want to talk like that, go where the man is. We don't want that kind of language used here, in the presence of our women and children."

Tooly, standing erect, high in his stirrups, drew a large pistol from its holster and swung it above his head.

"I will say what I please, where I please; and I don't care who likes it," roared Tooly, waving his pistol in air.

W. J. Van Diveer, a young man of the Drennan company, who had been sitting on a wagon-tongue near the speaker,

Van Diveer's advantage was slight, but sufficient

leaped to his feet, with a pistol levelled at the big horse-man's head, and with a manner that left no doubt that he meant what he said, shouted:

"I'll be damned if you can do that here. Now, you put down your gun, and go."

The muzzle of Van Diveer's pistol was within an arm's-length of Tooly, aiming steadily at his head. Tooly was yet with pistol in hand but not quite in position for use of it on his adversary. Van Diveer's advantage was slight, but sufficient for the occasion. Tooly's companions did not act, appearing to await his orders, and, in the suddenness of this phase of the scene, Tooly found no voice for commands. Others of our men made ready on the instant, believing that a battle was on.

It was averted, however. Tooly replaced his pistol in the holster, saying: "Well, of course—as you say, my pie is over yonder. I don't want to kill *you* fellows."

And he didn't. The three rode over to the other group of our men, among whom was Mr. Wood. All of these had overheard what had just been said, and felt sure they knew what was coming.

Mr. Wood, grief-stricken, disabled, stood, pale and fearful, amongst the party of timid emigrants, all strangers to him; he the only man probably in the camp without a weapon on his person, his torn arm in a sling across his chest.

The big fellow made his statement again, as he had made it to us; with the same emphatic threat to kill, if he could induce Wood or any one to speak out and affirm the charge of Tooly's complicity with the Indians.

Tooly got off his horse and, pistol in hand, walked among the party; many of whom surely did tremble in their boots. He declared again, as he stalked about, that he would shoot the hapless Wood, "like a dog", or any one who would repeat the charge.

There were but a few men in that part of the camp when Tooly commenced this second tirade, in the presence of Wood; but soon more came from the other part of the train.

Mr. Wood, in a condition as helpless as if with hands and feet bound, realizing his situation, and his responsibility, maintained silence: a silence more eloquent than speech, since a single word from him in confirmation of the charge he had made would have precipitated a battle, in which he, most certainly, and probably others, including some of his benefactors, would have been killed.

Then Tooly saw that a goodly number of men had arrived from the other section of the camp, and were watching to see what would happen; some of these viewing the scene with attitude and looks that boded no good for the man who held the centre of the arena.

Tooly's threatening talk ceased. Still Wood said nothing. In silence, Tooly mounted his horse, and with his fellows rode away, leaving the party of emigrants—most of them terror-stricken, some angry—standing dumb, looking at one another, and at the retreating three until they went out of sight, in the dusk of the desert night-fall: stood there on the sage-brush sward, a tableau of silent dumbfoundedness; for how long none knew; each waiting for something to break the spell.

"I feel like a fool," exclaimed Van Diveer.

"But," spoke Drennan, the older and more conservative leader of their party, "we couldn't start an open battle with those fellows without some of us being killed. They are gone; we should be glad that they are. It is better to bear the insult than have even one of our people shot."

"I'm glad they left no bullets in me—Ulee, ilee, aloo, ee; Courting, down in Tennessee."

This paraphrasing of his favourite ditty was, of course, perpetrated by "Jack."

But we all wished we knew. Was it true that these men were conspirators with the Indians who had been ravaging the emigrant trains? If so, doubtless they would be concerned in other and possibly much more disastrous assaults, and perhaps soon. If so, who would be the next victims?

But Mr. Wood was still too indefinite in his identification of the man Tooly—at least in his statement of it—to clear away all doubt, or even, as yet, to induce the majority of our men to act on the judgment of some: that we should follow these plainsmen, learn more, and have it out with them.

There were many circumstances pointing not only to the connection of these men with the assault on Mr. Wood's family, but to the probability of their having been responsible for the slaughter of the Holloway party. It seemed improbable that there were two bands of Indians operating along that part of the Humboldt River in the looting of emigrant trains. If it could be proved that white men cooperated with the savages in the Wood case, the inference would be strong that the same white men had been accessories in the Holloway massacre. The use of guns in those attacks, and the evident abundance of ammunition in the hands of the Indians, went far toward proving the connection of white men with both these cases.

CHAPTER 11

Sagebrush Justice

The Sink of the Humboldt is a lake of strong, brackish water, where the river empties into the natural basin, formed by the slant of the surrounding district of mountains, plain and desert, and where some of the water sinks into the ground and much of it evaporates, there being no surface outlet. In the latter part of the summer the water is at a very low stage, and stronger in mineral constituents. There we found the daytime heat most intense.

The land that is exposed by the receding water during the hottest period of the fall season becomes a dry, crackling waste of incrusted slime, curling up in the fierce sunshine, and readily crushed under foot, like frozen snow. The yellowish-white scales reflect the sunlight, producing a painful effect on the eyes. Not many feet wander to this forbidding sea of desolation.

At the border of this desert lake, a few feet higher than the water, is a plateau of sand, covered with sage-brush and stones. We were there in the last week of August. Fresh water was not to be had except at a place a half-mile from our camp, where there was a seepage spring. There we filled our canteens and buckets with enough for supper and breakfast. The animals had to endure the night without water.

Not far from the spring was situated a rude shack, known

as "Black's Trading Post." This establishment was constructed of scraps of rough lumber, sticks, stones and cow-hides. With Mr. Black were two men, said to be his helpers—helpers in what, did not appear. The principal stock in trade was a barrel of whisky—reported to be of very bad quality—some plug tobacco, and—not much else. Black's prices were high. A sip from the barrel cost fifty cents. It was said to be an antidote for alkali poisoning.

Some of our men visited this emporium of the desert, and there they found "Jim" Tooly. The barrel had been tapped in his behalf, and he was loquacious; appearing also to be quite "at home" about the Post. His two companions of our recent acquaintance were not there. The "antidote" was working; Tooly was in good spirits, and eloquent. He did not appear to recognize those of our people who were visiting the place; but they knew him. There were other persons present from the camps of two or three companies of emigrants, but strangers to us, who were also stopping for the night at the margin of the Sink.

Tooly assumed an air of comradeship toward all, address-

A SIP FROM THE BARREL COST FIFTY CENTS

ing various individuals as "Partner" and "Neighbour"; but his obvious willingness to hold the centre of the stage made it clear that he deemed himself the important personage of the community.

Some things he said were self-incriminating. He boasted of having "done up a lot of Pikers, up the creek," declaring his intention to "look up another lot of suckers" the following day.

When our men thought that they had heard enough they returned to camp and reported.

Recollections of the last time we had seen Mr. Tooly made the present occasion seem opportune. An impromptu "court" was organized: judge, sheriff and deputies; and these, with a few chosen men of the company, went to the trading post to convene an afternoon session. The members of this "court" dropped in quietly, one or two at a time, looked over the place, asked questions—about the country; the prices of Mr. Black's "goods"; how far it might be to Sacramento; anything to be sociable: but none offered to tap the barrel.

The stranger emigrants had heard of the Indian raids up the river. Seeming to have inferred something of pending events, they had gone to the trading post in considerable numbers. Tooly was still there. Black and his two men seemed to be persons who ordinarily would be classed as honest. Still, they appeared to listen to Tooly's tales of prowess in the looting of emigrant trains as if they regarded such proceedings as acts of exceptional valour; exhibiting as much interest in the recital as did the "tenderfoot" emigrants—who held a different opinion regarding those adventures.

When enough had been heard to warrant the finding of an indictment, the newly-appointed judge issued a verbal order of arrest, and the sheriff and his deputies quickly surrounded the accused, before he suspected anything inimical to his personal welfare. With revolver in hand, the sheriff commanded, "Hands up, 'Jim' Tooly!" To the astonishment of all, the big man raised both hands, without protest; this, however, in mock obedience, as was evident by his laughing at the supposed fun.

"This is not a joke, sir," came in harsh tones from the judge. "When we saw you last, about sixteen days ago, you came to our camp to deny a charge made against you by a man of our company. You overawed, browbeat and insulted the man and those who were assisting and protecting him in his distress. You denied the accusation made against you, with vehemence and much profanity. Giving you the benefit of a doubt, we permitted you to go. Now we are here to take the full statement of the prosecuting witness, and examine such other evidence as there may be. We will clear you if we can, or find you guilty if we must."

In whatever direction the culprit looked he gazed into the open end of a gun or pistol. The sheriff said:

"Now, Tooly, any motion of resistance will cost you your life."

A disinterested onlooker at the moment would have cringed, lest the unaccustomed duty of some deputy should so unnerve his hand that he would inadvertently and prematurely pull the trigger of his weapon. But all held sufficiently steady, as they looked through the sights.

The prisoner slowly grasped the situation, and knew that temporary safety lay in obedience. The sheriff's demand for Tooly's weapons created more surprise, when it was revealed that, in his feeling of security while at the Post, he had relieved himself of those encumbering articles and deposited them with the landlord, that he might have freedom from their weight while enjoying the hospitality of the place.

Thus his captors had him as a tiger with teeth and claws drawn. His weapons, when brought out from the hut for examination, were found to be two pistols, of the largest size and most dangerous appearance, in a leathern holster, the latter made to carry on the pommel of a saddle, in front of the rider. These, also his saddle and other trappings, were searched for evidence; but, except the pistols, nothing was found that tended to throw any further light on the question of his guilt or innocence.

Tooly was then taken, under a heavy guard, to a spot some distance from the Post, where the court reconvened, for the purpose of completing the trial.

His captors had, with good reason, reckoned Tooly as like a beast of the jungle, who, when put at bay, would resort to desperate fighting; but, having been caught thus unawares and unarmed, violence on his part or resistance of any kind, was useless. He was doubtless feigning meekness, hoping for an opportunity to escape.

A jury was selected, mostly from the stranger emigrants.

The improvised court sat on an alkali flat near the margin of the lake, where there were some large stones and clumps of sage-brush. There Tooly was confronted by Mr. Wood, still with bandaged arm. Tooly declared he had never before seen the Englishman, but Wood said he had seen Tooly, and now reaffirmed his belief that the prisoner was one of the persons who, some weeks previously, had ridden with the Indians who killed Mrs. Wood and the child, also wounded and robbed the witness.

Still the evidence was not deemed sufficiently positive or complete, the identity being in some doubt. The jury would not convict without conclusive proof. With the view of procuring further evidence, the judge ordered that the person of the prisoner be searched.

Hearing this mandate, Tooly first made some sign of an

intention to resist—only a slight start, as if possibly contemplating an effort to break through the cordon of untrained guards.

"Gentlemen," ordered the sheriff, "keep, every man, his eye on this fellow, and his finger on the trigger." Then to the prisoner,

"Stand, sir, or you will be reduced to the condition of a 'good Indian'!"

Escape as yet appeared impossible, and Tooly must have finally come to a definite realization that he was in the hands of men who meant business, most earnestly. Bravado had ceased to figure in his conduct. It was apparent that the search for evidence was narrowing its field; the erstwhile minions of frontier justice were on the right scent. Tooly grew pallid of feature and his cheeks hollowed perceptibly, in a moment. There was a wild glare in his eyes, as they turned from side to side; fear, hatred, viciousness, mingled in every glance. He crouched, not designedly, but as if an involuntary action of the muscles drew him together. His fists were clenched; his mouth partly opened, as if he would speak, but could not.

Thus he stood, half erect, while the officer searched his clothing. The examination disclosed that, secured in a buckskin belt, worn under his outer garments, there was English gold coin, to the value of five hundred dollars; just one-third of the amount that Mr. Wood declared he had lost at the time of the robbery. What became of the other two-thirds of Mr. Wood's money was readily inferred, but full proof of it was not necessary to this case.

Tooly's trial was closed. The only instruction the court gave the jury was, "Gentlemen, you have heard the testimony and seen the evidence; what is your verdict?"

The answer came, as the voice of one man, "Guilty."

During the entire proceeding, at the post and down by

'STOP,' SHOUTED THE JUDGE

the lake, the judge sat astride his mule. Addressing the prisoner once more from his elevated "bench," he said:

"Mr. Tooly, you are found guilty of the murder of Mrs. Wood and her child, the wounding of Mr. Wood, and robbery of his wagon. Mr. Wood has from the first stated his belief that you were with, and the leader of, the band of Indians which attacked his party. You afterwards denied it; but now, in addition to his almost positive identification, and many circumstances pointing to your guilt, you are found with the fruits of that robbery on your person. Have you anything to say?"

Tooly was ashy pale, and speechless. Absolute silence reigned for a time, as the court awaited the prisoner's reply, if by any means he could offer some explanation, some possible extenuating circumstance, that might affect the judgment to be pronounced. None came, and the judge continued:

"You can have your choice, to be shot, or hanged to the uplifted tongue of a wagon. Which do you choose?"

Tooly took the risk of immediate death, in seeking

one last, desperate chance for life. Instantly he turned half around, crouched for a spring, and, seemingly by one single leap, went nearly past the rock-pile, so that it partly covered his retreat. Quick as his movements were, they were not swifter than those of the men whose duty was to prevent his escape.

"Stop, Tooly," shouted the judge, sitting astride his mule, as his long right arm went out to a level, aiming his big Colt's revolver at the fleeing man.

"Shoot, boys," commanded the sheriff at the same instant; a chorus of shots sounded, and the court's sentence was executed.

Complying with the request of the judge, the sheriff had a hole dug near where the body lay, and the dead man was buried, *sans ceremonie*.

The court returned to the trading post and requested the proprietor to state what he knew of Tooly. Mr. Black declared he only knew that the accused plainsman came to the post that day; that he bought and drank a considerable quantity of whisky, and offered to treat several passing emigrants, all of whom declined.

The English gold found upon the prisoner was returned to Mr. Wood, and the incident was closed.

The trial had been as orderly and impartial as the proceedings in any court established by constitutional authority. All those concerned in it realized that they were performing a duty of grave importance. There was nothing of vindictiveness, nothing of rashness. It was without "due process," and it was swift; a proceeding without the delays commonly due to technicalities observed in a legal tribunal; but it was justice conscientiously administered, without law—an action necessary under the circumstances. Its justification was fully equal to that of similar services performed by the Vigilance Committee, in San Francisco, within a year preceding. It was a matter the necessity of which was deplorable, but the execution of which was imposed upon those who were on the spot and uncovered the convincing facts.

CHAPTER 12

From Arid Wastes to Limpid Waters

From the Sink of the Humboldt the little Darby party wished to complete the trip by the Carson Route, thus separating from the majority, but their supplies were exhausted and they had now but one ox and one cow to draw their wagon. A suggestion, that those who could spare articles of food should divide with the needy, was no sooner made than acted upon. Sides of bacon, sacks of flour and other substantials were piled into their little vehicle, and the owners of the two oxen which had been loaned Darby simply said, "Take them along; you need them more than we do." Danny, alias "Gravy" Worley, being of that party, showed his delight, by sparkling eyes and beaming fat face, when he saw the abundance of edibles turned over to his people. Mr. Darby shed genuine tears of gratitude, as we bade them good-bye and drove away by another route.

The combination train was further divided, each party shaping its farther course according to the location of its final stop. The Drennans took the Carson Route, the Maxwell train proceeding by the more northerly, Truckee, trail. The associations of the plains, closer cemented by the sharing of many hardships and some pleasures, had created feelings almost equal to kinship, more binding than those of many a life-long neighbourhood relation. So there were deep regrets at parting.

On leaving the Sink of the Humboldt there was before us a wholly desert section, forty miles wide. The course led south-westerly, over flat, barren lands, with a line of low hills, absolutely devoid of vegetation, on our right. This was known to be one of the hard drives of our long journey; but hearsay knowledge was also to the effect that, at its farther border, we would reach the Truckee River, and soon thereafter ascend the Sierra Nevada Mountains. The prospect of seeing again a river of *pure* water, and fresh, green trees, had a buoyant effect on our lagging hopes; and these were further stimulated by the information that not long after entering these forest shades we would cross the State line into California.

While crossing the forty miles of desert, the sun-baked silt, at the beginning, and later the deep, dry sand, made heavy going. To avoid the almost intolerable heat of day as much as possible, and it being known that water was not obtainable, during this much-dreaded bit of travel, we deferred the start until mid-afternoon, and travelled all night.

The impressions of that night ride were most extraordinary. As the sun sank, and twilight shaded into night, the atmosphere was filled with a hazy dimness; not merely fog, nor smoke, nor yet a pall of suspended dust, but rather what one might expect in a blending of those three. Only a tinge of moonlight from above softened the dull hue. It was not darkness as night usually is dark. It was an impenetrable, opaque narrowing of the horizon, and closing in of the heavens above us; which, as we advanced, constantly shifted its boundary, retaining us still in the centre of the great amphitheatre of half-night. We could see one another, but beyond or above the encompassing veil all was mystery, even greater mystery than mere darkness. No moon nor stars visible; nothing visible but just part of ourselves, and ours.

As the night merged into morning, the sunlight gradually dispelled the mantle of gloom from our immediate presence; but still we could not see out. As if enclosed in a great moving pavilion, on we went, guided only by the tracks of those who had gone before.

In the after part of the night the loose cattle, having been for two nights and a day without water, and instinctively expecting an opportunity to drink, quickened their pace, passing the wagons; the stronger ones outgoing the weaker, till the drove was strung out two or three miles in length along the sandy trail.

Some of the wise-heads in the company were fearful that the cattle, on reaching the Truckee River, would drink too much. They detailed Luke Kidd and me to ride on our mules ahead of the foremost of the stock, and on reaching the river, permit none of the animals to drink more than a little water at a time.

We went ahead during all that long morning, following what was surely, to us, the longest night that ever happened, before or since. Most of the other members of our party were in the wagons, and they, except the drivers, slept soundly; rocked gently, very gently, by the slow grinding of the wheels in the soft, deep sand. But Luke and I, on our little mules, must keep awake, and alert as possible, in readiness to hold back the cattle from taking too much water.

From midnight to daybreak seemed a period amounting to entire days and nights; from dawn till sunrise, an epoch; and from sunrise to the time of reaching the river, as a period that would have no end.

As the sun finally rose behind us, the faintest adumbration of the nearest ridges of the Sierras was discerned, in a dim, blue scroll across the western horizon, far ahead—how far it was useless to guess; and later, patches of snow about the peaks.

The minutes were as hours; and their passing tantalized us: noting how the dim view grew so very slowly into hazy outlines of mountains, and finally of tree-tops.

On we laboured, overcoming distance inch by inch; nodding in our saddles; occasionally dismounting, to shake off the almost overpowering grasp of sleep.

Half awake, we dreamed of water, green trees, and fragrant flowers. Rising hope, anon, took the place of long-deferred fruition, and we forgot for a moment how hard the pull was; till, with returning consciousness of thirst and painful drowsiness, we saw the landscape ahead presented still another, and another line of sand-dunes yet to be overcome.

Luke and I reached the Truckee at nine o'clock in the forenoon, just ahead of the vanguard of cattle, and about three miles in advance of the foremost wagon.

We tried to regulate the cattle's consumption of water, but did not prevent their drinking all they could hold. Ten men, on ten mules, could not have stopped one cow from plunging into that river, once she got sight of it, and remaining as long as she desired. We could not even prevent the mules we rode from rushing into it—that cold, rippling Truckee. Yet our elders had sent us two boys to hold back a hundred cattle, and make them drink in instalments—in homeopathic doses, for their stomachs' sake.

They dashed into the stream *en masse*; and seeing the futility of interfering, we gladly joined the cattle, in the first good, long, cool swallow of clear, clean water, within a period of six weeks.

Our little mules did not stop till they reached the middle of the river, and stuck their heads, ears and all, under the water. Luke's diminutive, snuff-coloured beast was so overcome by the sight and feel of water that she lay down in it, with him astride, giving herself and her master the first real bath since the time that she did the same thing, in the Platte River, some three months previously.

To us, the long-time sun-dried, thirsty emigrants; covered from head to foot with dust from the Black Hills, overlaid with alkali powder from the Humboldt, veneered with ashes of the desert; all ingrained by weeks of dermatic absorption, rubbed in by the wear of travel, polished by the friction of the wind—to us said the Truckee, flowing a hundred feet wide, transparent, deep, cool; rattling and singing and splashing over the rocks; and the sparkle of its crystal purity, the music of its flow and the joy of its song, repeated, "Come and take a drink."

We filled our canteens and went back to meet the others. We found them in a line three miles long; and it was well into the afternoon when the last wagon reached the river.

The train crossed to the farther shore, into the grateful shade of the pine forest and there made camp.

What an enchanting spectacle was that scene of wooded hills, with its varying lights and shades, all about us! From as far as we could see, up the heights and down to the river bank, where their roots were washed in the cool water, the great trees grew.

We were still within the confines of Nevada, but two men were there with a wagon-load of fresh garden stuff, brought over from the foothills of California to sell to the emigrants: potatoes, at fifty cents a pound, pickles, eight dollars a keg, and so on. We bought, and feasted.

The camp that night by the Truckee River was the happiest of all. We had reached a place where green things grew in limitless profusion, where water flowed pure and free; and we were out of the desert and beyond the reach of the savage Redman.

CHAPTER 13

Into the Settlements

Having begun the ascent of the lofty and precipitous east slope of the Sierra Nevada Mountains, one night about the first of September the camp-site selected was at a spot said to be directly on the boundary line between Nevada and California.

Lounging after supper about a huge bonfire of balsam pine, the travellers debated the question whether we were really at last within the limits of the Mecca toward which we had journeyed so patiently throughout the summer. While so engaged, the stillness, theretofore disturbed only by the murmur of our voices and occasional popping of the burning logs, was further dispelled for a few seconds by sounds as of shifting pebbles on the adjacent banks, accompanied by rustling of the foliage, waving of tall branches and tree-tops, and a gentle oscillation of the ground on which we rested. These manifestations were new to our experience; but we had heard and read enough about the western country to hazard a guess as to the significance of the disturbance.

"Jack," aroused from his first early slumber of that particular evening, raised himself on an elbow, and asserted, confidently:

"That settles it; we *are* in California: that was an earthquake."

Appearing already to have caught the universal feeling of western people regarding the matter of "quakes," he chuckled, in contemplation of his own perspicacity, and calmly resumed his recumbent attitude, and his nap.

The summit of the Sierras was reached within about two days from the commencement of the ascent. We met no people in these mountains until we had proceeded some distance down the westerly slope, and reached a mining camp, near a small, gushing stream, that poured itself over and between rocks in a tortuous gorge.

The camp was a small cluster of rough shacks, built of logs, split boards and shakes. As if dropped there by accident, they were located without regard for any sort of uniformity. These were the bunk cabins of the miners; some of the diminutive structures being only of size sufficient to accommodate a cot, a camp-stool and a wash-basin. A larger cabin stood at about the centre of the group, the joint kitchen and dining-room.

MELICAN MAN DIG GOLD

As we drove into the "town," the only person within view was a Chinaman, standing at the door. For most of us this was a first introduction to one of the yellow race. He was evidently the camp cook.

Major Crewdson approached the Celestial with the salutation: "Hello, John."

"Belly good," was the reply.

Having already heard it said that the invariable result of an untutored Chinaman's effort to pronounce any word containing an "r" produced the sound of "l" instead, we thought little of that error in the attempt of this one to say "Very," but believed that his substitution for the initial letter of that word was inexcusable.

"What is the name of this place?" continued Crewdson.

"'Melican man dig gold."

"Yes, I know that; but, this town, what do you call it?"

"Yu-ba Dam," the Chinaman answered.

This response was intended to be civil. Near by the Yuba River was spanned by a dam, for mining purposes, known as Yuba Dam, which gave the mining camp its name.

Further on we came to the first house that we saw in California; and it was the first real house within our view since the few primitive structures at Nebraska City, on the west shore of the Missouri River, faded from our sight, the preceding spring. During a period of about four months our company had travelled thousands of miles, through varying wilds, in all of which not one habitation, in form common to civilization, had been encountered. Seldom has civilized man journeyed a greater distance elsewhere, even in darkest Africa, without passing the conventional domicile of some member of his own race. Long ago such an experience became impossible in the United States.

This house was a small wayside inn, situated where a miners' trail crossed the emigrant route; a roughly-made,

PACK-MULE ROUTE TO PLACER DIGGINGS

two-story, frame building, with a corral adjoining; at which mule pack-trains stopped overnight, when carrying supplies from Sacramento and Marysville for miners working the gold placer diggings along the American and Yuba rivers. We camped beside the little hotel, and the next morning were for the first time permitted to enjoy a sample of the proverbially generous California hospitality, when the landlord invited our entire company into his hostelry for breakfast.

Our entrance into California was in Nevada County, thence through Placer, Sacramento, Solano and Napa, and into Sonoma.

Over the last one hundred miles we saw evidences that the valleys, great and small, were rapidly filling with settlers.

The last stream forded was the Russian River, flowing south-westerly through Alexander Valley, to the sea. Having crossed to the western shore, our motley throng found itself in the settlement embracing the village of Healdsburg, an aggregation of perhaps a dozen or twenty houses. There our worn and weather-stained troop made its final halt; and the jaded oxen, on whose endurance and patient service so much—even our lives—had depended, were unyoked the last time, on September seventeenth, just four months after the departure from the Missouri River.

Considering all the circumstances of the journey, through two thousand miles of diversified wilderness, during which we rested each night in a different spot; it seems providential that, on every occasion when the time came for making camp, a supply of water and fuel was obtainable. Without these essentials there would have been much additional suffering. Sometimes the supply was limited or inferior, sometimes both; especially during those trying times in the westerly portion of the Humboldt region; but we were never without potable water nor fire, at least for the preparation of our evening meal. Nature had prepared the country for this great overland exodus from the populous East; a most important factor in the upbuilding of the rich western empire, theretofore so little known, but whose development of resources and accession of inhabitants since have been the world's greatest marvel for more than half a hundred years.

As I look back, through the lapse of nearly sixty years, upon that toilsome and perilous journey, notwithstanding its numerous harrowing events, memory presents it to me as an itinerary of almost continuous excitement and wholesome enjoyment; a panorama that never grows stale; many of the incidents standing out to view on recollection's landscape as clear and sharp as the things of yesterday. That which was worst seems to have softened and lapsed into the half-forgotten, while the good and happy features have grown brighter and better with the passing of the years.

Whether pioneers in the most technical sense, we were early Californians, who learned full well what was meant by "Crossing the Plains."

ALSO FROM LEONAUR

WELLINGTON AND THE PYRENEES CAMPAIGN VOLUME I: FROM VITORIA TO THE BIDASSOA *by F. C. Beatson*—The final phase of the campaign in the Iberian Peninsula.

WELLINGTON AND THE INVASION OF FRANCE VOLUME II: THE BIDASSOA TO THE BATTLE OF THE NIVELLE *by F. C. Beatson*—The second of Beatson's series on the fall of Revolutionary France published by Leonaur, the reader is once again taken into the centre of Wellington's strategic and tactical genius.

WELLINGTON AND THE FALL OF FRANCE VOLUME III: THE GAVES AND THE BATTLE OF ORTHEZ by *F. C. Beatson*—This final chapter of F. C. Beatson's brilliant trilogy shows the 'captain of the age' at his most inspired and makes all three books essential additions to any Peninsular War library.

NAVAL BATTLES OF THE NAPOLEONIC WARS *by W. H. Fitchett*—Cape St. Vincent, the Nile, Cadiz, Copenhagen, Trafalgar & Others

SERGEANT GUILLEMARD: THE MAN WHO SHOT NELSON? *by Robert Guillemard*—A Soldier of the Infantry of the French Army of Napoleon on Campaign Throughout Europe

WITH THE GUARDS ACROSS THE PYRENEES by *Robert Batty*—The Experiences of a British Officer of Wellington's Army During the Battles for the Fall of Napoleonic France, 1813.

A STAFF OFFICER IN THE PENINSULA *by E. W. Buckham*—An Officer of the British Staff Corps Cavalry During the Peninsula Campaign of the Napoleonic Wars

THE LEIPZIG CAMPAIGN: 1813—NAPOLEON AND THE "BATTLE OF THE NATIONS" *by F. N. Maude*—Colonel Maude's analysis of Napoleon's campaign of 1813.

BUGEAUD: A PACK WITH A BATON by *Thomas Robert Bugeaud*—The Early Campaigns of a Soldier of Napoleon's Army Who Would Become a Marshal of France.

TWO LEONAUR ORIGINALS

SERGEANT NICOL by *Daniel Nicol*—The Experiences of a Gordon Highlander During the Napoleonic Wars in Egypt, the Peninsula and France.

WATERLOO RECOLLECTIONS by *Frederick Llewellyn*—Rare First Hand Accounts, Letters, Reports and Retellings from the Campaign of 1815.

ALSO FROM LEONAUR

AVAILABLE IN SOFTCOVER OR HARDCOVER WITH DUST JACKET

THE JENA CAMPAIGN: 1806 *by F. N. Maude*—The Twin Battles of Jena & Auerstadt Between Napoleon's French and the Prussian Army.

PRIVATE O'NEIL *by Charles O'Neil*—The recollections of an Irish Rogue of H. M. 28th Regt.—The Slashers— during the Peninsula & Waterloo campaigns of the Napoleonic wars.

ROYAL HIGHLANDER *by James Anton*—A soldier of H.M 42nd (Royal) Highlanders during the Peninsular, South of France & Waterloo Campaigns of the Napoleonic Wars.

CAPTAIN BLAZE *by Elzéar Blaze*—Elzéar Blaze recounts his life and experiences in Napoleon's army in a well written, articulate and companionable style.

LEJEUNE VOLUME 1 *by Louis-François Lejeune*—The Napoleonic Wars through the Experiences of an Officer on Berthier's Staff.

LEJEUNE VOLUME 2 *by Louis-François Lejeune*—The Napoleonic Wars through the Experiences of an Officer on Berthier's Staff.

FUSILIER COOPER *by John S. Cooper*—Experiences in the 7th (Royal) Fusiliers During the Peninsular Campaign of the Napoleonic Wars and the American Campaign to New Orleans.

CAPTAIN COIGNET *by Jean-Roch Coignet*—A Soldier of Napoleon's Imperial Guard from the Italian Campaign to Russia and Waterloo.

FIGHTING NAPOLEON'S EMPIRE *by Joseph Anderson*—The Campaigns of a British Infantryman in Italy, Egypt, the Peninsular & the West Indies During the Napoleonic Wars.

CHASSEUR BARRES *by Jean-Baptiste Barres*—The experiences of a French Infantryman of the Imperial Guard at Austerlitz, Jena, Eylau, Friedland, in the Peninsular, Lutzen, Bautzen, Zinnwald and Hanau during the Napoleonic Wars.

MARINES TO 95TH (RIFLES) *by Thomas Fernyhough*—The military experiences of Robert Fernyhough during the Napoleonic Wars.

HUSSAR ROCCA *by Albert Jean Michel de Rocca*—A French cavalry officer's experiences of the Napoleonic Wars and his views on the Peninsular Campaigns against the Spanish, British And Guerilla Armies.

SERGEANT BOURGOGNE *by Adrien Bourgogne*—With Napoleon's Imperial Guard in the Russian Campaign and on the Retreat from Moscow 1812 - 13.

www.ingramcontent.com/pod-product-compliance
Lightning Source LLC
Chambersburg PA
CBHW032018090426
42741CB00006B/641